FILM

E 70

FILM
The Front Line 1984

BY DAVID EHRENSTEIN

ARDEN PRESS, INC.
Denver, Colorado
1984

ISBN 0-912869-05-4
ISSN 0740-1566

Typography by Van Bogart Graphics

Published in the United States of America
Arden Press, Inc.
1127 Pennsylvania
Denver, Colorado 80203

791.43
E 33

Publisher's Note

The Front Line is an annual series meant to bring a greater prominence to the work of experimental and personal filmmakers, whose access to the film press has been severely limited. The range of work is broad—from the barely narrative to the purely structural—but as the number of volumes increases we will try to move repeatedly along the edge of the art. The selection of artists to be covered in each volume will, of course, indicate the critical inclinations of the author, but by opening the series each year to a critic with a strong and personal view, we hope the series will begin to generate not only a broad portrait of the front line, but also a critical dialogue that will bring the political and aesthetic issues of the avant-garde into sharper focus.

The 1983 volume, by Jonathan Rosenbaum, remains available. (ISBN 0-912869-03-8; $10.95paper.)

The Front Line 1985, by Chuck Kleinhans, will be released in December 1985.

For Bill Reed,
and to the memory of Peter Blum

Operate on—excision
　　　　　make an excision
　　　　　make an excision in a text
　　　　　operate on a text through an excision
Cut oneself into the avant-lard

　　　　　　　　　　　—Jacques Ehrmann

Table of Contents

Acknowledgments

In addition to the filmmakers, the author would like to thank the following parties for their help and guidance: Gilbert Adair, Beth B, Jonathan Benair, Joan Cohen, Jim DiGiovanni, Mrs. Pearl Ehrenstein, Simon Field, Gary Graver, Robert A. Haller, Ronald Haver, Bill Krohn, Jonas Mekas, Richard Meltzer, Mark Rappaport, Jackie Raynal, Bill Reed, Jonathan Rosenbaum, and P. Adams Sitney.

Jack Smith and John Ahearn in *The Trap Door*, by Beth B and Scott B

INTRODUCTION

We all know why we're here. We all know what roles we're expected to play. In the theater of avant-garde and independent film study, writer and reader are well rehearsed. Names, dates, and running times are to be noted, thematic and formal properties described, historical precedents cited, and artistic hierarchies established. A time-honored tradition—logical, even useful in its way—it has been ceaselessly performed in books, specialized film journals, and academic quarterlies for decades. The only problem is that the ostensible subject remains as unexamined after the performance as it was prior to the moment when the curtain rose.

"Discourse about the cinema," writes Christian Metz in *The Imaginary Signifier*, "is too often part of the institution, whereas it should be studying it and believes or pretends that it is doing so." No question of the truth of this remark. On television would-be actors spout "opinions" of current releases, rarely deviating from a norm of hyperenthusiastic gush. Newspaper and magazine reviewers, overweeningly self-important in their offerings of yeas and nays, struggle to create an impression of critical authority and uncompromising high standards. But such posturings are undercut by a fundamental unwillingness to question the nature of the spectacles placed before them, or to consider the possibility of filmmaking—and filmgoing—alternatives. Comments—positive or negative—center solely on the efficacy of techniques designed to produce an emotional response in the viewer, never considering the meaning or purpose of such responses. All are part of what Metz calls "the third machine: after the one that manufactures the films and the one that consumes them, the one that *vaunts* them, that valorizes the product."

In the avant-garde and independent film arena the machine would appear to function along more modest lines—conscientious consideration replacing reflexive reaction. But then that aspect of the process is largely subsumed by the *a priori* value avant-garde and independent film has always claimed for itself. On one level the claim is perfectly justifiable. There is an obvious difference between small-scale individually executed works and enormous productions assembled by teams. But this difference is not in and of itself sufficient to constitute a genuine alternative to mass-market film practice. The machine is content to examine the formal and thematic concerns that separate avant-garde and independent works from the commercial mainstream, often seeing such differences as constituting in and of themselves a radical break with status quo film practice on every level (e.g. the writings of Peter Gidal). But when it comes to elucidating how this radicalism might function in relation to production, distribution, exhibition, or any other area where the cutting edge of cinematic difference could truly be tested the machine falls silent. An annotated list of achievements stretching across times, places, and the individual circumstances of the filmmakers involved, observed in pristine aesthetic isolation, is no substitute for genuine critical engagement. It is obvious that a common chain of concerns draws such otherwise diverse films as **Blood of a Poet**, **Meshes of the Afternoon**, and **Twice a Man** together. But concentration on artistic similarities alone risks reducing avant-garde and independent film from the status of an alternative to the mainstream to that of a mere sub-genre of it—which is by and large its actual status today.

Kristin Thompson's study of the work of Charles Dekeukeleire published in *Millennium Film Journal* (#7/8/9, Fall-Winter 1980-81) provides an example of the pitfalls of such machine-tooled critiques. On the surface her piece is a relatively well-reasoned account of the career of this Belgian experimental filmmaker—provided of course one can properly consider Dekeukeleire experimental at all. Thompson freely admits that only four of Dekeukeleire's 83 films can be seen in this context. Nevertheless, she's quite content to prattle on about the alleged glories of the four produced between 1927 and 1930—**Combat de boxe**, **Impatience**, **Histoire de detective**, and **Witte Vlam**—comparing them favorably to films by Duchamp and Léger made in the same period. There was no commercial film industry in Belgium at that time. There was, however, a flourishing Cine-Club along the lines of those in France that had propelled Buñuel, Cocteau, and many others to prominence. Thompson makes note of the complete independence Dekeukeleire enjoyed (he owned his own camera and lighting equipment), praising his "refusal to compromise." That "refusal" was short-lived, for in 1932 Dekeukeleire took a job with a French newsreel company (former avant-garde filmmaker Germaine Dulac was its director) for which he made a documentary about the Belgian Congo. From that moment until his death in 1971, documentary was Dekeukeleire's primary form.

"I have sampled a few of his documentaries," Thompson confesses, "and they have none of the fascination imparted by a Resnais or Marker. Rather they are exactly the kind of films a business firm, a national tourist board, or a charity hopes for when giving out a commission: well-made, reasonably interesting, unexceptional in both senses of that word." Thompson's assessment may be true enough. But then it wouldn't be entirely unreasonable to regard the quartet of experimental films Dekeukeleire made in the same manner—exactly the sort of works a Cine-Club owner hopes for when planning a season. Toying with narrative conventions (the thriller parody **Histoire de detective**), highlighting moments of pure abstraction (a set of blocks is listed as a featured player in **Impatience**), and even providing a soupçon of sex (a naked female motorcyclist appears in the same film—hot stuff for 1929), they're perfectly acceptable products of that system. Thompson herself notes in best industry-scribe fashion that **Combat de boxe** "received good reviews and ran for three months." Consequently, there is no need to speak of "compromise" at all. Dekeukeleire simply moved from one system to another. Thompson appears aware at some level that it is a system she's dealing with rather than an aesthetic disposition. "I think audiences accustomed to Snow, Conrad and structuralist filmmakers probably have a better preparation for Dekeukeleire's work than his contemporaries did," she claims. And she is doubtless correct; such audiences have become comfortably accustomed to that brand of "experiment" through its exposure in the museums, classrooms, and auditoriums that have replaced Cine-Clubs as purveyors of such products. What Thompson can't quite seem to realize is that it *is* product—that avant-garde and independent films are consumer commodities like any other.

A few years after the publication of this Dekeukeleire piece, another one, by critic J. Hoberman, appeared in *The Village Voice* (July 31, 1984) echoing Thompson's sentiments (with full acknowledgment of the latter's original insights). Hoberman's readership is, of course, different from Thompson's. Hers is on the look-out for research materials for future thesis papers; his is merely in the market for some slightly more off-beat form of diversion than found in the movie mainstream (its chief sphere of influence). In this context, Thompson's scholarly veneer appears a virtual guarantor of quality—an intellectual Seal of Approval as it were.

Hoberman does not content himself with a mere photocopy of Thompson's views. He goes her one step further, making a case for one post-"experimental" Dekeukeleire effort, **The Evil Eye** (1937). Dekeukeleire's sole non-documentary (of his non-avant-garde period), this melodrama set in the Flemish Ardennes is highlighted, according to Hoberman, by a flashback "so clogged with superimpositions as to be barely decipherable." Hoberman cites this sequence as some sort of avant-garde last stand on Dekeukeleire's part. But "experimental" bits presented in self-enclosed form in otherwise ordinary narratives (e.g. flashbacks, dream sequences, drug and alcohol hallucinations) were standard operational procedure in the Thirties and Forties. Vaunted "experimental" filmmaker/theorist Slavko Vorkapich carved a career out of the manufacture of such montages, which largely served as an artistic elephant's graveyard for innovations seen on the Cine-Club circuit a decade before. This utilitarian construct crippled avant-garde film practice for over a decade, placing the complexities of Eisenstein, Vertov, and many others under the rubric of visual window-dressing.

Taking Dekeukeleire's early films out of mothballs and clothing them in new "structural" clothes is a continuation of this practice. Seen in this light, the avant-garde pivots solely on surface tics and effects, suffering no alteration on any fundamental level from one era to the next, and consequently having no real impact on the way films are produced or consumed.

"We must dismiss everything he did for money; and we must value what he made as art," writes P. Adams Sitney of filmmaker Dimitri Kirsanoff,* who like Dekeukeleire began his career in an "experimental" mode in the late Twenties. Certainly it's not unreasonable to find certain works of this Russian-born filmmaker (who made his career in France) superior to others— depending on what standards are being used. Kirsanoff may indeed have had more creative control over those of his films that Sitney prizes (**Menilmontant, Brumes d'automne, Rapt**) and thus affords a special status. Still, it doesn't follow that his other films (Sitney does not mention their names) are of necessity entirely worthless—their value may very well be of another degree, like Dekeukeleire's documentaries. But that's not what's behind the *ipso facto* superiority of "money" to "art" emphasized here—seeking as it does to distinguish that which Kirsanoff "did" from what he "made." Obviously, this "art" requires financing in order to be realized, but the means of its doing so are no concern of Sitney's, nor is the profit to be made from it. Such concern would risk destroying "art's" ... value—sullying it with aspects of vulgar commerce.

Unexplored, therefore, is the commercial status that "art" has always enjoyed—the world of film included. A **Raiders of the Lost Ark** can produce an enormous, immediate return on its investment; a **Serene Velocity** cannot possibly hope to command such profits. Profit participation proceeds, nonetheless, along somewhat different lines. Such films are grist for the academic and institutional mills that have come to be considered the proper province of all that is best in avant-garde and independent work today. There are papers to be written about them, courses to be taught, lectures to be given. Once a film's importance in that sphere is firmly established, there are museums and university film libraries that may wish to purchase prints. Overseeing the entire process are such commercial concerns as the Chase Manhattan Bank, the Exxon Corporation, Consolidated Edison, the Minolta Corporation, Agfa-Gavaert, et al., all only too eager to benefit from the tax advantages and advertising goodwill contributions to this non-profit network provide. Still, there's a need to go through with the charade of rejecting "money" and embracing "art" as both are inextricably linked on every conceivable level. Drawing attention to such processes might impede their flow. No question that the workers involved will do anything to avoid embarrassing their bosses. In the world of the commercial film it isn't unusual to hear of directors referred to (or referring to themselves) as whores. In the

---

*In Richard Roud, ed., *Cinema: A Critical Dictionary* (New York: Viking, 1980), pp. 551-553.

same spirit it would therefore not be inappropriate to take note of the pimps of Academe, laboring tirelessly at the behest of the *maison close* of culture.

The potential for avant-garde and independent film to make a difference—to become a genuine alternative—has always been clear. Writing of audience reactions to early screenings of Jack Smith's **Flaming Creatures**, filmmaker Gregory Markopoulos noted viewer delight at the discovery of "those images, scenes and sequences which they had envisioned and had wished would appear in the commercial films which they attended."* Filmmakers could thus oppose Hollywood by situating themselves tangentially to it—playing on the excesses and absences of its long-established currents of cinematic desire.

For a time this method served as an exceedingly viable tool. Naturally enough attendant on its successful application was an awareness of avant-garde and independent film's commodity status. And for a time there was a de facto acknowledgment of this. Jonas Mekas's weekly column in *The Village Voice* provided a prime channel of publicity for the movement—denigrating the commercial mainstream while encouraging readers to try something newer, smaller, more personal, and more unusual in its stead. Moviegoers of every stripe had good reason to consider his suggestion, as avant-garde and independent film had by then become synonymous with sexual daring and social rebellion.

But as a once-timid Hollywood started to accommodate itself to screen sexuality the picture altered. When hardcore pornography emerged as a separate industry with its own exhibition and distribution system, the erotic novelty that had served as avant-garde and independent film's secret selling point was no longer viable. Aspects of social upheaval had begun to lose their attractiveness as well with the end of the Vietnam war. Soon a once despised "selling out" metamorphosed into a thoroughly acceptable procedure of "buying in."

A formerly free-wheeling avant-garde and independent film scene was now dominated by the "structural" sub-genre (the films of Snow, Gehr, Frampton, etc.), which emerged as a paradigm of proper form. No ambiguity as to what these films were "about," pivoting as they did on concepts relevant to philosophy, phenomenology, linguistics, and mathematics. Soon legitimization by the art establishment (up to now most reluctant to concede links between such figures as Stan Brakhage and Jackson Pollock) came in the form of special issues of *Artforum*. In short, the machine was now running full tilt, and any attempt at disruption of its processes was sure to meet with severe censure.

"It's about time that film scholars disabuse themselves of the fantasy that they are on the barricades," chides Noel Carroll,† "we are a

---

*"Innocent Revels," *Film Culture* #33 (Summer 1964), pp. 41-45.

†"Art, Film and Ideology: A Response to Blaine Allan," *Millennium Film Journal* #13 (Fall-Winter 1983-84), p. 120.

comparatively tiny enclave addressing each other and not the proletariat." One would hope that those few proletariat who for some reason or another chanced to pick up that issue of *Millennium Film Journal* would have had the decency—for Carroll's sake at the very least—to drop it from their hands on reaching the above line and to return to reading matter more suitable to them—the career of Michael Jackson perhaps. No doubting the fact that we are no longer on the barricades due to such energetic efforts to segregate culture along class lines.

Avant-garde and independent film still holds the promise of an alternative, both in relation to the commercial marketplace (which ignores it), and the academic establishment (committed to embalming it). To keep that promise alive, however, it is necessary to put everything—films, filmmakers, audiences, critics, and exhibition practices—constantly to the test. An area that in the last decade has been comfortably charted out must be examined—and re-examined. This book can only attempt to take a very small step in that general direction. Consisting as it does of essays devoted to the work of filmmakers (complete with filmographies and running times—a small but by no means decisive concession to the institutional model, for reasons that will shortly become clear), it can offer only a select portion of a much larger picture. In a way that serves as an advantage. The filmmakers dealt with here—American and European—are in no way linked together in some vast seamless ensemble. Some of them, by current academic standards, might be considered irrelevant and unimportant—which no doubt they are as far as institutional purposes are concerned. Their presence in this context pivots on the way they have attempted (with varying degrees of success) to make a difference in the face of the two establishments that presently hold sway. This is simply a first foray—one of many excisions to be made if film of any kind is to have any meaning.

JACK SMITH.
Born in Columbus, Ohio, 1932.

1961—*Scotch Tape* (16mm, color, 3 min.)
1963—*Flaming Creatures* (16mm, b&w, 45 min.)

Note: Outside of the two works listed above, no other films by Jack Smith exist in the finite form generally deemed suitable for filmographic reference purposes. Between 1963 and 1964 Smith executed principal photography on *Normal Love*, a film that he has since continued to edit into differing versions under a number of titles, the most recent being *Tales of Cement Lagoon* and *Normal Fantasy*. In 1967 Smith presented a selection of his shorter works under the title *Horror and Fantasy at Midnight*. 1969 saw the appearance of *No President* (also known as *Slave President* and *The Kidnapping and Auctioning of Wendell Wilkie by the Love Bandit*), which, like *Normal Love*, has since been dismantled and reassembled in numerous ways. Sheldon Renan's "An Introduction to the American Underground Film" (Dutton, 1967) makes note of an unfinished Smith work shot between 1951 and 1956 entitled *Buzzards Over Baghdad*, a 1960 opus *Overstimulated*, and *In the Grip of the Lobster Claw*, identified as his then current project. The Filmmakers' Cooperative's "Lecture Bureau Catalogue #1" lists a 1969 Smith film, *Loathsome Kisses of Bagdad*. Smith's 1972 *Village Voice* article on *Reefer Madness* mentions *Zombie of Uncle Pawnshop* (no date given) as one of his works. Smith screenings are by and large one-time-only affairs, featuring footage both new and old in different assemblages under an ever-changing array of titles (e.g. a 1981 unspooling in San Francisco—*Lucky Landlordism of Lobster Lagoon*). He distributes and exhibits his own films. He also performs slide shows and theatrical works.

Mrs. Alving: *(beaming with pleasure)* I know one who has kept both the inner and the outer man free from harm. Just take a look at him, Mr. Manders.

Oswald: *(walks across the room)* Yes, yes, mother dear, of course.

Manders: Undoubtedly—no one can deny it. And I hear you have begun to make a name for yourself. I have often seen mention of your name in the papers—and extremely favorable mention, too. Although, I must admit, latterly I have not seen your name so often.

—Henrik Ibsen, *Ghosts*, Act I

The American avant-garde *is* Jack Smith. Filmmaker, actor, playwright, photographer, illustrator, he has for over three decades produced less a "body of work" of comfortably definable contours than a radical aesthetic of perpetual fluidity and incalculable influence. Placing the marginal front and center, granting power to the culturally dispossessed, Smith has developed an artistic vision of unprecedented authority. In his hands discarded film stock turns to a mine of visual riches, amateur players disclose depths no "professional" could hope to reveal, decor culled from pieces of (literal) garbage vibrate with scenic loveliness, and executional errors, rather than distract, reveal themselves as the essence of affectivity. In short, aesthetic parameters are inverted with Smith, as decisively as moral ones are with Jean Genet. But in place of that French master's religious paradigm of saint and criminal becoming as one, Smith offers another form of iconic interplay in the person of B-movie siren Maria Montez.

"Her eye saw not just beauty, but incredible, delirious, drug-like, hallucinatory beauty," Smith wrote of his celluloid beloved in his seminal theoretical study "The Perfect Filmic Appositeness of Maria Montez" (*Film Culture* #27, Winter 62/63). To Smith no words of praise were too great for this Dominican Republic-born star (1919-1951) whose sultry poker face graced a clutch of cheap romantic adventure fantasies churned out by Universal pictures in the mid-to-late Forties. "Corniness is the other side of marvelousness," Smith declared in his Montez paen, finding in such films as **Ali Baba and the Forty Thieves**, **White Savage**, and **Cobra Woman** vital links to a hidden history of the cathartic power of the aesthetically disreputable: "The whole gaudy array of secret-flix, any flic we enjoyed: Judy Canova flix (I don't even remember the names), *I Walked With a Zombie, White Zombie, Hollywood Hotel* ... most Dorothy Lamour sarong flix, a gem called *Night Monster, Cat & the Canary, The Pirate*, Maureen O'Hara Spanish Galleon flix (all Spanish Galleon flix anyway), all Busby Berkeley flix, *Flower Thief*, all musical production numbers, especially Rio de Janeiro prod. nos., all Marx Bros. flix. Each reader will add to the list."

Today pop movie cults and "bad" film connoisseurs abound. Smith's words, however, were penned prior to Susan Sontag's signal discovery of "camp." Pauline Kael dismissed Smith as a bad joke, using his Montez insights to attack Andrew Sarris in her famous "Circles and Squares" broadside (in *I Lost It at the Movies*, Atlantic/Little-Brown, 1965, p. 314)—Smith representing the furthest extremes of the *auteur* theory. In other circles, however, Smith's ideas were taken far more seriously. Arising in the early Sixties was a whole generation of post-beat artisans whose notions of style as substance were entirely beholden to Smith's views—especially as regards the creative projection of personality.

"I'D RATHER HAVE ATROCIOUS ACTING," Smith claimed. "Acting to Maria Montez was hoodwinking. Her real concerns (her convictions of beauty/her beauty) were the main concern—her acting had to be secondary. An applying of one's convictions to one's activity obtains a higher excellence in that activity than that attained by those in that activity who apply the rules established by previous successes by others." As diffuse as such ideas may seem on the printed page, they were clear to Smith's followers. Ordinary standards of performing excellence were restrictive. By such standards Maria Montez "failed." As *herself* however—a vibrant personality with methods and mannerisms of her own idiosyncratic making—she succeeded. From this basic principle the "Theater of the Ridiculous" in its multifarious manifestations (the plays of Ronald Tavel, John Vaccaro, Charles Ludlam, and Kenneth Bernard) was born. With its love of parody, exhibitionism, personal eccentricity, sexual vulgarity, and old movies—particularly old Maria Montez movies—the "Ridiculous" movement left its mark on the theatrical scene in a way that is still felt today. It stands as but one example of Smith's influence.

"How many people who are so-called leaders of the American experimental theater owe volumes to Jack Smith?" American experimental theater leader Richard Foreman asked in a *Village Voice* interview (January 2, 1978). Both Foreman and avant-garde spectacle *maestro* Robert Wilson culled much from Smith's theoretical ideas and visual designs for their temperamentally cooler concoctions. Wilson even went so far as to attempt to repay his debt by casting Smith in his mammoth theatrical epic "Deafman Glance," whose mammy-infested rainforests and crumbling Egyptian temples would scarcely have been out of place before Smith's cameras. It is the perspective of the camera that separates Smith from his theatrical progeny in the last analysis. For as wide a shadow as Smith cast over the avant-garde theater, it is as nothing compared to his catalyzing effect on the film scene.

Throughout the 1960s (simultaneous with the unfolding of the theater movements mentioned above) Smith placed his stamp as a performer (and on occasion creative collaborator) in the films of Ken Jacobs (**Blonde Cobra, Star Spangled to Death**), Ron Rice (**Chumlum, The Queen of Sheba Meets the Atom Man**), Andy Warhol (**Dracula, Hedy**), and many others. The center of Smith's power, however, radiated from a work that was his alone, **Flaming Creatures**—the most important avant-garde film ever made in America.

Flaming Creatures, by Jack Smith

Shot on backdated black-and-white stock over a series of weekends on the roof of a soon-to-be demolished theater (and in Smith's apartment) at the cost of a mere $300, **Flaming Creatures** exemplifies the bohemian daring and homoerotic imaginativeness that are the true roots of the American avant-garde. On a blandly objective level **Creatures** consists of little more than 45 plotless minutes in which a group of men—mainly transvestites—and a few women, pose, dance, playfully paw at one another, and occasionally display an exposed breast or limp penis. On the soundtrack throughout the action one can hear the strains of such *outré* pop-corn as "Amapola," "Siboney," and "Be-bop-a-lu-la" interspersed with bits of idle chatter (something about a new heart-shaped lipstick) plus a few wisecracks. The total effect of the film, however, is less difficult to describe directly.

Placing his figures (none can be called actors in the generally accepted sense of the term) against a (mainly) stark white backdrop, completely destroying dramatic film's usually well-defined sense of fore- and background and up and down (much of **Creatures** was shot with Smith standing on a ladder, his cast splayed out on the floor beneath him), Smith cocktails-up *tableaux vivants* that appear simultaneously planned and accidental. Figures jut into the frame at odd angles emphasizing both the discretion of individual camera set-ups and the enormity of the off-screen space surrounding them. No single figure takes charge as Montez did in her films, though a blonde-wigged transvestite (Joel Markman) does a bit of solo flower clutching that has been much commented on in analysis of the film (with comparisons frequently made to Marilyn Monroe). As Smith's creatures group together and break apart, suggestions of a party or parade scene hang in the air—as if the entire movie were some sort of "second unit" take to be edited into some other more conventional production later on. Even in what might be called the climax, when the action takes on the form of a mock orgy (frenzied clutching and grabbing, one of the women screaming in terror and/or ecstasy) followed by an earthquake (Smith's camera pitching and heaving about like a drunken sailor), things quickly dissipate, disintegrate, and collapse into inertia. Everything about the film appears elusive and indistinct, even the time of its making, as the backdate stock (blazing whites cut through with shades of charcoal gray predominate) contrives to make **Creatures** appear a film of the 1930s.

What Smith was driving at with all of this can best be seen through a passage from one of his short stories, "The Memoirs of Maria Montez or Wait for Me at the Bottom of the Pool" (*Film Culture* #31, Winter 63/64):

> The scaffolding around the Vapid Lot slipped. It rumbled and crumbled but didn't fall to the ground. More scaffoldings would be constructed around the crumbling scaffolding to keep it up. But the weight of the old scaffolding would weaken the new scaffolding and another crust of scaffolding would be built around

the whole. Long ago the Movie Studio itself had fallen and now only repetition memories filmed themselves there. But the walls could never be located to be rebuilt if anyone cared to look as no one did because they had fallen into a powder among the maze of scaffolding. And the scaffolding was thick; it provided a thick wall of green darkness behind which the entire lot strove incessantly to create a film the name and subject of which was forgotten long ago, strove as in an endless hopeless dream to attempt to start to try to start this film with no personnel, a leading man dying of old age, a dead leading lady, a decomposing beloved old character actress, no leadership or funds, or coffee money but certain gorgeous color rouged subjective images and a couple of marvelous fantasticated, Etruscated, ruined sets.

In literature there are precedents for such baroque convulsive nostalgia; not just European writers like Genet, Kafka, and Baudelaire (the latter far too glibly evoked *vis-à-vis* Smith), but Americans like William Burroughs, Nathaniel West, Alfred Chester, Robert M. Coates, and Irving Rosenthal. On film, however, there was and is no point of comparison. To a heretofore staid American avant-garde, rife with tenth-rate imitations of Jean Cocteau and Twenties-era surrealism, Smith was a rude awakening.

Smith was confident there was an audience ready, even eager, for the sort of experience **Flaming Creatures** provided. In the late Fifties and early Sixties he had witnessed the growth of an adventurous movie-viewing atmosphere at the now-legendary experimental film screenings at the Charles Theater on New York's lower east side. In contrast to Cinema 16, then the most established experimental venue, the Charles screenings were in Smith's words "wide open" with audience members free to project whatever caught their fancy on the big Charles screen. Smith was hopeful this sort of spectator/spectacle interplay could continue through his work. But by the time **Creatures** was completed, the Charles (for which he had specifically designed the film) had changed its policy. **Flaming Creatures** made its debut at the Gramercy Arts theater, to the delight of the bohemian *cognoscenti*. But another factor that would alter Smith's career forever was beginning to enter the picture.

"I started making a comedy about everything I thought was funny," Smith recalled of **Creatures** in a 1978 interview with Sylvère Lotringer,* "and it *was* funny. The first audiences were laughing from the beginning all the way through. But then *that writing* started—and it became a sex thing.... There was dead silence in the auditorium." No denying the film's humor. No denying its matter-of-fact sexual adventurousness either. In the context of its time there was no way it could have passed unnoticed. Whether

---

*"Uncle Fishook and the Sacred Baby Poo-Poo of Art," *Semiotext (e)* VIII, no. 2 (1978), p. 192.

the sexual frankness of **Creatures** would have created quite the sensation it did had attention not been specifically drawn to it, however, is another question. For today, there is no way of talking about **Flaming Creatures** without dealing with "that writing" to which Smith takes such vocal exception.

"There is very little hope that Smith's film will ever reach the movie theater screen," Jonas Mekas declared in his "Movie Journal" column in *The Village Voice* after attending a preview screening. "This movie will be called pornographic, degenerate, homosexual, trite, disgusting. It's all that and it is so much more than that," hardly suggestive of a work containing so much as the barest trace of humor—or of one likely to endear itself to the police authorities once it *did* reach the movie theater screen. As for the "more than that" of which Mekas spoke, critic Ken Kelman was among the first to spell out its details, on the pages of *Film Culture* (#29, Summer 1963)—and it was no laughing matter either: " ... the very scope and scale of sin becomes demonic in a Miltonian sense ... a paen not for the Paradise lost, but for the Hell Satan gained." Rather drastic stuff, but pretty much par for the course in the way it feeds on the occult sub-strain of the American avant-garde (Maya Deren, Kenneth Anger, Harry Smith, etc.). Smith, for his part, was flabbergasted by such analogies, going so far as to take a course in witchcraft at the New School in order to find out just what he had reportedly been up to.

Aleister Crowley cultism to one side, there was more to the avant-establishment's interest in **Flaming Creatures** than simple cultural consumption. By the time of the Third International Experimental Film Exposition at Knokke-Le Zoute in Belgium, Smith's film had been transformed into a weapon in an ongoing, attention-getting anti-censorship crusade. When the festival's selection committee objected to **Flaming Creatures** on the grounds that its brief views of exposed genitalia might be in violation of an obscure Belgian law, Mekas resigned from the Knokke festival jury in protest.

"I myself am not so sure about what really happened at Knokke during that stormy, confused, disappointed, sad, desperate week," Mekas declared in his column. Filmmaker James Broughton struck a calmer tone in his coverage of the event in *Film Quarterly* (Spring 1964), noting that **Flaming Creatures** "became the most discussed and most often shown film at the festival" as a result of Mekas's screening it in his hotel room to any and all interested parties practically round-the-clock. Further, according to Broughton, festival director Jacques Ledoux quickly "became delighted by the whole scandal, [and] executed the *coup de grace* by awarding the film a special prize 'maudit.' "

Knokke was scarcely the limit of the film's new-found notoriety. "Two minutes after I met Federico Fellini in Rome," a flabbergasted Stanley Kaufmann reported, "he asked me whether I'd seen Jack Smith's **Flaming Creatures**." Susan Sontag penned a laudatory article on Smith's film, hailing it "a triumphant example of an aesthetic vision of the world" and correctly recognizing its true subject as "joy and innocence" (in *Against Interpretation*, Farrar, Straus, and Giroux, 1966). But Sontag's insights weren't about to be shared by police authorities who, rising to the bait of pornographic promise, turned their attention away from the likes of Lenny Bruce to arrest this fantasy representation. Trials, fines, and legal hassles of all sorts followed, keeping a film that, while seen by few, had gained the status of a household word, out of circulation for a decade.

Smith, by this time, had turned his artistic attention elsewhere. Immediately upon completion of **Creatures** he had begun production on a color epic briefly referred to as **The Great Pasty Triumph**, then **Normal Love**.

Normal Love, by Jack Smith

Armed with backdate color stock, his usual stable of transvestite stars (Frances Francine, Mario Montez) plus some new-to-Smith players (Diane De Prima, Andy Warhol, and a then-unknown Tiny Tim), he set off for the wilds of New Jersey. Dressing some of his cast members as horror-movie archetypes (the Mummy, the Werewolf) he invented new personas of his own devise for others (a mermaid, a spider-woman, a white bat). The rushes from **Normal Love**'s three main production shoots (two were outdoors in swamps and forests, one was executed in Smith's studio/loft) were like nothing seen before or since. The backdate color gave the images a rich other-worldly hue, augmented by Smith's uncanny sense of costume and decor. Numerous screenings of bits and pieces of this sumptuous epic (the longest assemblage being some 90 minutes of footage) were arranged. But **Normal Love** never achieved the final form **Flaming Creatures** did. Even more than its predecessor, this Smith work was a succession of dramatic fragments. Instead of suggesting any sense of cohesion, each scene (and sometimes each shot) emerged as a self-enclosed entity with an affective power all its own. A brightly lit sequence of creatures dancing in the open air on an enormous cake (a parody/hommage of sorts to both Browning's **Freaks** and Busby Berkeley's "No More Love" production number from **Roman Scandals**) seemed to compete in impact with other scenes such as a subtler darker-toned one of a mummy in dream-like pursuit of a cobra woman (actress Beverly Grant with a snake wrapped around her neck) in a wood at twilight. Soon Smith began experimenting with his film in other ways, changing the order of sequences and changing the music and sound effects on the tapes he used to accompany screenings. The image of breakdown and regeneration underscored in the passage of his writing quoted earlier had now become a principle of his art, continuing in his work subsequent to **Normal Love**— **Horror and Fantasy at Midnight** and **No President**. Smith was slowly bringing to film the spontaneity and sense of intemporality common to the theater. In the last decade his work in film (which has seen **Normal Love** transformed into **Tales of Cement Lagoon** and **Normal Fantasy**), theater, and slide show presentations suggests some sort of synthesis of the entire process. There are no clear dividing lines with Smith as to where one form of activity begins and another ends—all three spill over into one another constantly.

Smith's 1977 production of Ibsen's "Ghosts" entitled "The Secret of Rented Island" is especially revealing of his ideas along this line. As described by Stefan Brecht in his book *Queer Theatre* (Suhrkamp Verlag, 1978), Smith's work is enacted in a set consisting of bits of drapery, a moorish archway, heaps of dust and glitter, and items of middle-class home furnishing. Smith (starring as Oswald) and his cast declaim bits and pieces of the text as if at rehearsal. At the outset of the run, some of the supporting players were human (e.g. an old transvestite named "Monty Carlo" played Mrs. Alving) while other roles were enacted by inanimate objects manipulated by a small child (a stuffed pink pig as Regina, a toy monkey as Pastor Manders). With much of the dialogue tape-recorded in advance, everything proceeded much as in Japanese puppet theater. As the play's run continued, however, Smith took over more aspects of the performance himself, with other players gradually dropping away. In its final incarnation, "The Secret of Rented Island" featured Smith alone, manipulating the light and sound effects, moving the toys and objects about, and reading all the parts. This performance, however, shouldn't be seen as the final outcome of his labors—the intended destination in a process of paring the production away to its essence. The paring itself is Smith's play. There is no finality here, no product, only process—a continual working through. Space for such work was throughout the 1970s becoming in short supply.

In an article in *The Village Voice* (December 21, 1972), Smith gave public airing to resentments that had been smoldering semi-privately for some time. The article was a review of the late Thirties exploitation film **Reefer Madness**, an unintentionally hilarious warning against the perils of marijuana use that in 1972 had become a cult classic. Midnight moviegoers at New York's Elgin theater were responding to the film with an enthusiasm Smith hadn't seen since the glory days of the Charles. Because of **Reefer Madness**'s less-than-feature length, the Elgin management had seen fit to add another short and a Betty Boop cartoon to the program. Smith hailed the show as "a burst of generosity in these stingy times," contrasting it with the exhibition practices of what now constituted the avant-garde. Letting fly at Jonas Mekas, Smith called his past champion "more a Rona Barrett than a Savonarola but less a guru than a praying mantis," and claiming he (Mekas) was "able to go from co-op to pawnshop in 10 easy years." In another *Voice* article published sometime later (a review of **Pink Flamingos** in the July 19, 1973 issue) Smith was even more vociferous in his anti-Mekas blasts, referring to the critic/filmmaker as a "Golden Brassiere Publicity Mummy" who gave others "useless tidbits of information then blurbed them in print and sponged off the baby-vomit of art, while taking the opportunity to slip the museum price tag of death around the neck of each."

To a film public that had for years almost routinely saluted what Susan Sontag in her **Flaming Creatures** review called "the tenacity, even heroism of Jonas Mekas," this was all something of a shock. Hadn't Mekas risked fines and imprisonment for Smith's sake? Weren't these simply the ravings of a disgruntled talent whose era had passed? Perhaps, but closer examination reveals more than a grain of truth to Smith's charges. Simply put, the press and legal attention brought to **Flaming Creatures** put the American avant-garde on the map. No longer would it be the interest of a fixed group of isolated acolytes; now it would face the public at large as a new, exciting, and sexually daring alternative to Hollywood. Countless other experimental filmmakers found it possible to ride into public view on **Creatures**'s coattails. As Smith's experimentation moved him outside the publicity pale, Andy Warhol arrived on the scene to take up the slack—his avant-garde ascendancy reaching its climax with the unexpected commercial success of **The Chelsea Girls**. For one brief moment it looked as if the avant-garde might be able to square off against the commercial cinema on the same public footing.

But as the Seventies arrived everything changed. Warhol abandoned the avant-garde for ordinary commercial venues, the bohemia he exposed in **The Chelsea Girls** converted—with the help of director Paul Morrissey—into the formula farce of **Trash** and **Heat**. No one emerged from the avant-garde as his successor—a figure capable of capturing both the headlines and the mass public's fancy. The once all-important war against censorship was now not so much won as forgotten, as pornography took its place as a legal consumer service—thus depriving the avant-garde of its commercial cutting edge. Filmmakers were no longer displaying their wares in small theaters and Cine-Clubs alone, but in museums and archives—the "non-commercial" province of what President Reagan refers to as the "private sector." No wonder the form avant-garde filmmaking had taken was calmer, cooler, and more emotionally distant. No wonder a premium was now being placed on the finite as opposed to the anarchic. All these works had to be catalogued, appraised, and properly analyzed by the critical overseers inextricably wedded to this new form of institutionalization. Naturally enough, there was no place for Smith in any of this. "I have a roomful of films," he said in the Lotringer interview, "but there's nothing in the world that I can do with them because Uncle Fishook [Mekas] has established this pattern of the way film is thought about and seen, and everything else."

The truth of Smith's remarks is borne out, albeit inadvertently, in the introduction to a recently published book, *The Baudelairean Cinema—A Trend within the American Avant-Garde*, by Carel Rowe (UMI Research Press Studies in Cinema, 1982). As might be expected from the title, Rowe is in full support of the standard academic line on Smith, placing him (along with Warhol, Anger, Rice, and several others) within the context of the nineteenth-century symbolist tradition. The novel aspect of Rowe's research is her disclosure of information concerning the two and one-half months she spent in New York with Smith, "tailing him around town, filming, videotaping, and assisting him with his 'Sharkbait of Atlantis' slide show." One would think from this that Rowe would have gained some sympathetic understanding of Smith's means and ends. But instead she bewails her inability to wrest "much coherent material" from him, complaining to Jonas Mekas of the "difficulty involved in any attempt to communicate verbally" with Smith. Seeing Smith's severing of relations with Mekas as tantamount to his rejection of writers of any kind, Rowe voices "terror of being discovered as a critic/scholar, a 'mekasite' double agent." This evidently was indeed the case as she goes on to say that she "certainly never questioned Mekas's position in keeping the negative out of Jack's destructive clutches." The situation reached a climax according to Rowe when Smith discovered Mekas, P. Adams Sitney, and Annette Michelson in the audience at one of his slide shows. "He accused me of bringing them to 'spy' on his shows and banished the four of us from the theatre, screaming that he would murder Jonas if he wrote a word about what he'd seen there that evening." Despite this burst of energy Rowe relates that "after the scene at the Jane Street theatre, he [Smith] seemed finally to shut himself off—not only from critics but from the necessity (or ability) to give performances or make films."

To anyone who has kept abreast of Smith's activities over the past few years—film and slide shows, theater productions, acting appearances in works like Beth B and Scott B's **The Trap Door**—or met him in person, Rowe's appraisal is something of a surprise. But in light of the fact that Rowe is clearly beholden to what the avant-establishment has to make of Smith, it's less surprising. Smith has his place clearly laid out for him in the grand artistic/historical scheme. P. Adams Sitney in *Visionary Film* (Oxford University Press, 1978) marks it plainly. Smith belongs to the "mythopoeic stage" of the movement's development—something on the order of a passing adolescent episode en route to the full-blown artistic maturity of Brakhage, Frampton, et al. Sitney awards Smith high marks for his "visions of liberated consciousness," praises his visual flair, notes the possible influence of the (culturally respectable) Joseph Cornell (Smith was duly impressed by the sculptor/filmmaker's **Rose Hobart**), and recounts in some detail the history of Jonas Mekas's involvement with Smith and the brand of bohemia from which he sprang. The bottom line, however, is something else again. "The question that his [Smith's] performance provokes," Sitney declares, "is how conscious is he of turning these apparently neurotic activities into an aesthetic strategy?" Sitney concludes on the basis of Smith's performance piece "Rehearsal for the Destruction of Atlantis" that Smith "is aware of the effect of his methods," but the overall impression persists, nonetheless, of an artist too rarified, too disorganized, and too marginal to be granted ultimate serious consideration.

It would be nice to be able to bypass all of this bitterness and backbiting, all of these resentments and personal squabbles, and look at the work itself. But no work can be looked at for itself. It carries along with it the marks left by history—by what others have made of it. **Flaming Creatures** began its existence as a work by Jack Smith. Over the years it has become something more—and for that reason to some degree something less—than what he made. To get at the *real* **Flaming Creatures**—a film still possessed of enormous power—requires a willingness to slash away at the critical and journalistic barnacles with which it has become encrusted. The same can't be said of the rest of Jack Smith. It—he—remains elusive and ever-changing, a constant reproach to the status quo, the bottom line of everything that wishes to call itself avant-garde.

. . . the argument thus far

Jack Smith virtually embodies the crisis in avant-garde and independent film practice today. By going against the avant-establishment grain he has risked rendering himself a cultural non-person—a fact underscored by a review of Carel Rowe's book which came to the conclusion from the evidence offered that Smith had *died*.* This is a far more serious situation than that outlined by Jonathan Rosenbaum in the previous volume of this series.

The critical mainstream's indifference to non-industrial products is perfectly understandable as it functions solely at the behest of consumers who compose one segment of the urban upper-middle class. Those in thrall to such scribes, consequently, cannot be excused as misguided or uninformed. Their class allegiance is inextricably tied to a disposition toward cultural conformity. As for those critics and moviegoers venturing off beaten commercial pathways, understanding what is to be found there is largely dependent on a willingness to come to grips with *all* the processes involved. Unquestioned acceptance of the institutional ghetto only serves to perpetuate its power—a power every bit as absolute as that of the mass market. Admittedly, this puts everyone—filmmakers, critics, and moviegoers alike—on the line. But as Smith's case indicates, that is precisely where everyone is to begin with, for like all else in culture it comes down to a question of politics—a fact underscored in this instance by the avant-establishment's insistence on Smith's apoliticality.

"He was floating around in that kind of reality," claimed Jonas Mekas of Smith at the time of **Flaming Creatures**. "He was obsessed with that reality; he had to do it, and he did it with his friends. It had nothing to do with any politics; it was his world, the life that he lived." The avant-establishment's unwillingness to conceive of lived experience in political terms is well known. But it gets a particular twist with Smith in light of the clearly homosexual vision that **Flaming Creatures** puts on display. Categorized as an "obsession" the sexual is thus kept apart from the political.

---

*Howard Davis, *On Film* #12 (Spring 1984), p. 55. Davis's conclusion was corrected in a subsequent issue of the journal.

Smith is quite clear about his point of view. "Basically I'm an anarchist," he declared in a *Semiotext(e)* interview.* "Anarchy is the giving part of politics. In this country they have stamped it out, and made it a dirty word, made it synonymous with chaos.... They want to tell you that it's the same thing as chaos. It isn't. All it means is without a ruler. And if people don't try to make a start of getting along without authorities, they will never be in a position where they are not being worked over by these authorities."

KEN JACOBS.
Born in New York City, 1933.

1956—*Orchard Street* (16mm, b&w, 15 min.)
1957—*Saturday Afternoon Blood Sacrifice: TV Plug: Little Cobra Dance* (16mm, color and b&w, 9 min.)
1960—*Star Spangled to Death* (16mm, color and b&w, 120 min., unfinished)
1961—*Little Stabs at Happiness* (16mm, color, 18 min.)
 The Death of P'Town (16mm, color, 7 min.)
1962—*Blonde Cobra* (16mm, color and b&w, 28 min.)
 Film material by Bob Fleischner and Jack Smith. Composed by Ken Jacobs.
1963—*Baud'larian Capers* (16mm, color and b&w, 30 min.)
1964—*Window* (16mm, color, 12 min., silent)
 The Winter Footage (8mm, color, 40 min., silent; blown up to 16mm in 1984)
 We Stole Away (8mm, color, 40 min., silent; blown up to 16mm in 1984)
1965—*Lisa and Joey in Connecticut: "You've Come Back!" "You're Still Here!"* (8mm, color, 20 min., silent)
 Naomi Is a Vision of Loveliness (8mm, color, 4 min., silent)
1966—*The Sky Socialist* (8mm, color, 120 min., unfinished; to be blown up to 16mm and completed in 1984)
1967—*Air Shaft* (16mm, color, 4 min., silent)
1968—*Soft Rain* (16mm, color, 12 min., silent)
1969—*Tom Tom the Piper's Son* (16mm, b&w and color, 118 min., silent; revised in 1971)
 Nissan Ariana Window (16mm, color, 21 min., silent)

---

*"Uncle Fishook and the Sacred Baby Poo-Poo of Art," *Semiotext(e)* III, no. 2 (1978), p. 192.

1973—*Changing Azazel*
1974—*Excerpt from the Russian Revolution* (16mm, b&w,
        20 min.)
1975—*Urban Peasants* (16mm, b&w, 40 min.)
1976—*Spaghetti Aza*
1978—*The Doctor's Dream* (16mm, b&w, 25 min.)

Film/Performance Works
1965—*The Big Blackout of '65: Chapter One, "Thirties
        Man"*
1966—*The Big Blackout of '65: Chapter Two, "Slide of
        the City"; Chapter Three, "Naomi Is a Dream of
        Loveliness"*
1968—*The Big Blackout of '65: "Evoking the Mystery"*
1970—*Restful Moments* (3-D)
1972—*A Good Night for the Movies (II): 4th of July by
        Charles Ives by Ken Jacobs*
1974—*A Man's Home Is His Castle Films: The European
        Theater of Operations*
        " 'Slow Is Beauty'—Rodin" (two- and three-dimen-
        sional shadow play)
1975—*The Boxer Rebellion*
        The Impossible: Chapter One, "Southwark Fair"
1976—*Flop: 4th of July, 1976*
1977—*"Air of Inconsequence"*
1979—*Ken Jacobs at the Console Performing "Stick to Your
        Carpentry and You Won't Get Nailed"*
        The Impossible: Chapter Two, "1896"
1980—*The Impossible: Chapter Three, Schilling; Chapter
        Four, Hell Breaks Loose; Chapter Five, The Wrong
        Laurel*
        C X H X E X R X R X I X E X S (3-D)
1981—*Ken Jacobs Theater of Unconscionable Stupidity
        Presents Camera Thrills of the War* (3-D)
1982—*The Whole Shebang* (3-D)
1983—*Making Light of History: "The Philippines
        Adventure"* (3-D)
        Ken Jacobs films are available from the Film-Makers' Cooperative.

One of the most annoying habits in critical analysis is the tendency to
reduce an artist to the size of a single work. Orson Welles made other—better—films than **Citizen Kane**. Jean Renoir likewise neither begins nor ends
with **The Rules of the Game**. And so it goes with Ken Jacobs and **Tom Tom
the Piper's Son**. There is no way of ignoring the brilliance of this delightful
piece of meta-cinema. But the status **Tom Tom** has held for over a decade

as its creator's principal achievement has resulted in obscuring the breadth and depth of a truly remarkable body of work. Part of the reason this situation has come about has to do with the establishment of the structural sub-genre—a category under which **Tom Tom** was instantly (and not entirely justifiably) subsumed. But critical fashions to one side, perception of **Tom Tom** as pivotal provides Jacobs's career with the one feature it most conspicuously lacks—a solid center. It is certainly possible to find formal links and recurring themes across the wildly diverse span of Jacobs's work, concerns that appear to meet in **Tom Tom**. But what *separates* each Jacobs film from the next is often more compelling than what joins them. Consequently, less than a focal point, **Tom Tom the Piper's Son** can be more usefully regarded as a provisional outpost—a locus of some, but not all, of Jacobs's interests.

This said, **Tom Tom** is still as good a place as any to begin a discussion of Jacobs's achievements. Made from a 10-minute 1905 film (attributed to D. W. Griffith's cameraman G. W. "Billy" Bitzer) depicting the well-known nursery rhyme in eight highly theatrical scenes, Jacobs's film is stretched to feature length by the refilming and (more important) reframing of its action. Using several procedures to transform the original spectacle—including slow and stop motion, masking areas of the screen, creating frames within frames by filming the screen from an angle, moving the camera across

Tom Tom the Piper's Son. Ken Jacobs. Still courtesy Anthology Film Archives.

otherwise static shots to create a sense of panning and tracking—Jacobs makes *another* film. But while different in kind, this new **Tom Tom** is similar in fundamental effect. We see everything that was there originally but in greater detail as Jacobs's cropping of the screen (creating what he has called a "Griffith emphasis") and regulation of movement give separate visual events (a man tumbling, a woman playing with a hoop, people climbing a ladder, Tom running with his stolen pig) editing-table intimacy.

"My camera closes in, only to better ascertain the infinite richness," Jacobs has written in the Film-Makers' Cooperative catalog, "(playing with fate, taking advantage of the loop-character of all movies, recalling with variations some visual complexes again and again for particular savorings), searching out incongruities in the story-telling (a person, confused, suddenly looks out of an actor's face), delighting in the whole bizarre human phenomena of story-telling itself and this within the fantasy of reading any bygone time out of the visual crudities of film: dream within a dream!" In short, in a gesture both modest and magisterial, Jacobs underscores the visual richness all film is heir to. We are thus invited by Jacobs, in a most casual manner, to read between the lines of culture.

Arriving when it did in 1969, however, **Tom Tom the Piper's Son** wasn't about to be seen in a low-key light. An entire matrix of critical preoccupations had emerged by then, involving not only the notion of structural cinema, but also the opposition to narrative that was seen as the avant-garde's chief goal. However, the question of whether **Tom Tom** truly belonged in such a context was gradually glossed over. Critics Lois Mendelson and Bill Simon, in their lengthy analysis of the film for *Artforum* (September 1971, vol. X, no. 1), were perfectly justified in comparing *some* aspects of Jacobs's approach to Dziga Vertov's in **The Man with the Movie Camera**. But the use of similar devices (e.g. stop and slow motion) shouldn't be confused with similar purposes. Vertov rejected the entire concept of narrative. Jacobs is clearly interested in it—**Tom Tom** "has to do with a member of the tribe coming into sexual maturity, and the way it is greeted by the tribe."* Aspects pertaining to deconstruction are likewise difficult to apply to Jacobs's project as the 1905 original film (in a manner not at all uncommon to works of its era) is in no way comprehensible as a "story" in the sense of the term generally accepted today. Without prior knowledge of the "plot" (i.e. the theft of the pig) the film appears largely as directionless frenzy at a crowded fairground. Jacobs himself admitted, "I saw the film many times before I knew there was a pig." In this sense, Jacobs's version creates a *stronger* narrative than the one that existed originally, even to the point of adding new dramatic material: " … in the section where the woman on the tightrope does this waving of the handkerchief, and then kissing. She blows a kiss to

---

*"An Interview with Ken Jacobs," by David Shapiro, *Millennium Film Journal*, vol. 1, no. 1.

someone in the audience. I directed the kiss to Tom, by cutting in a shot of him doffing his cap."

P. Adams Sitney (who pulls out all the high culture stops comparing Jacobs's film to Manet, Stravinsky, and Picasso) is closer to the mark in citing the influence of Joseph Cornell's **Rose Hobart**. Taking a relatively routine early Thirties melodrama, Cornell (in contrast to Jacobs) *reduced* its length to that of a short. Rearrangement of the film's cutting continuity also entailed the adding of shots from other sources. The resultant film directs our attention toward those random moments of dramatic affectivity that impress the viewer on a non-narrative level (e.g. the stance of the figure, the flair of a gesture, the texture of the light) but that are swallowed up in a conventional context by story sense. We see the leading lady (Rose Hobart), pensively pacing a room, lounging about a garden, glancing off-screen toward things we aren't shown (as Cornell's editing has eliminated them), reacting to words we can't hear (Cornell's film has music but no dialogue). From these "privileged moments" (François Truffaut's useful term) a new layer of affectivity is revealed. Hobart in Cornell's hands is transformed into that person who "suddenly looks out of an actor's face." This methodological transformation naturally enough relates to another figure as crucial to Jacobs as Cornell—Jack Smith.

"Images always give rise to a complex of feelings, thoughts, conjectures, speculations, etc.," wrote Smith apropos Maria Montez—"remarkable for the gracefulness of her gestures and movement. This gracefulness was a real process of moviemaking."* The fact that such gracefulness was to be found in works devoid of genuine artistry proved to be a further source of fascination to both filmmakers. "We both became interested in shit," Jacobs recalled, "and the energy that was allowed when you come to the junctures of shit … mindless banal crap could break open and give off fantastic aesthetic energy."†

The late Fifties and early Sixties saw Jacobs and Smith working together on a number of projects tangential to such "shit" energy, the most important being **Star Spangled to Death**. A massive assemblage of improvised routines featuring Smith and actor Jerry Sims, plus bits and pieces of home movies, industrial shorts, and other "found" material, this deliberately shapeless epic would appear to be set on capturing the same brand of bohemian *zeitgeist* seen in **Pull My Daisy**, which was made more or less around the same time. Jacobs's film, however, quickly shows itself concerned with realms of experience far beyond that of Robert Frank and Alfred Leslie's now-classic "beat" charade. In **Star Spangled to Death** not only are Smith's and Sims's semi-symbolic seriocomic antics recorded (lavishly childlike traipsing about indoors and out in Greenwich Village and points lower east),

---

*"The Perfect Filmic Appositeness of Maria Montez," *Film Culture* #27 (Winter 1962/63), p. 28.
†Unpublished interview in the files of the Anthology Film Archives.

but their by-products are as well—retakes, accidents, false starts, lunch breaks, interruptions, etc. This obsession with the artistic outer limits logically extended itself to post-production. The film was originally shown in work print form in the hopes of raising money for its completion. But everyone involved instantly recognized that the stops, starts, and breakdowns accompanying such projections completed on some level the gesture first advanced in the film's making—an infernal machine of production, destruction, and regeneration.

This is not to say that Jacobs (who intends to put **Star Spangled to Death** into some sort of definitive shape in the near future) was willing to go as far as Smith in eliminating all notions of finality. For during the same period of all-stops-out movie madness he also made **Little Stabs at Happiness**. Just 18 minutes long, this delicate mood piece takes the form of a loose grouping of quasi-dramatic episodes separated by silent-movie style intertitles (e.g. "It began to Drizzle"). Each section succeeds in capturing what Jacobs has called "a few of those inexpressible moods of the moment." Jack Smith plays (semi-lasciviously) with a doll. Jerry Sims sits in meditative calm. Jacobs himself makes a chalk drawing on a sidewalk. Such scenes could easily have been woven into the rapid-fire texture of **Star Spangled to Death**. Here they float—discrete moments delicately placed against a backdrop of

Little Stabs at Happiness. Ken Jacobs. Still courtesy Anthology Film Archives.

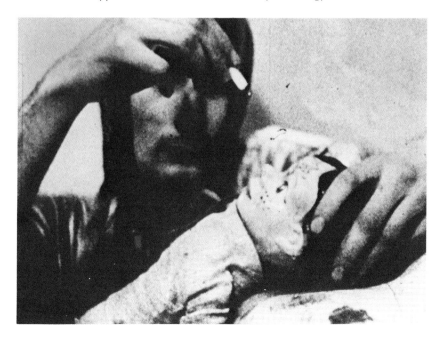

obscure old pop tunes and bits of narration in which Jacobs (gently, haltingly) describes what we're seeing and how it came to be there. **Little Stabs at Happiness** slides ever so subtly about moments of sadness and melancholy without ever alighting on them. These fragments never quite become scenes or character sketches, yet they don't lapse into coy symbolism either. Jack Smith may be identified as the "spirit of listlessness," but the label is lightly worn. "Strictly light summer fare," Jacobs has written of the film, "very easy and fun to do." Naiveté and sophistication here co-exist without one cancelling the other out.

This same dialectic figures in three entirely different Jacobs works, **Window**, **Air Shaft**, and **Soft Rain**, short silent works that form a loose trilogy. Made up of precisely what their titles suggest, these visual studies appear in one sense to show how little one can put on the screen and still have a film. Jacobs plays with the elements of light and shadow, shape and texture, and the like in a manner nudging up against areas explored by (among others) Stan Brakhage and Ernie Gehr. But the phenomenological rapture of the former and the calculated rigor of the latter don't figure here. These are visual subjects that might have been discovered by the people we see in **Little Stabs**. Nominally abstract, they resist the dryness generally associated with the "structural" works they are usually associated with as they carry the force, if not the aspect, of drama.

This same subtlety is even more marked in Jacobs's 8mm films, particularly **We Stole Away** and **Lisa and Joey in Connecticut: "You've Come Back!" "You're Still Here!"** The first concerns a summer spent by Jacobs and his family in Southhampton, Long Island. The second revolves around Alfred Leslie and his family in New York City. Both are in a surface sense simple homemovies. Yet the tone Jacobs discovers here is not so easily categorized. We see outdoor vistas, figures walking through the streets and (occasionally) pausing before the camera in snapshot-like repose—the stuff of "amateur" cinema. The treatment, however, is clinically cool—as if it were all documentation to be gathered for some *future* use.

The homemovie as folk artifact has always fascinated Jacobs. In the early Sixties, he featured at screenings of his own films homemovies taken of his friends Artie and Marty Rosenblatt by their uncle when the pair were children. Like the "shit" of commerce, these films have no pretense to art, yet they produce an artistic afterglow. The filmmakers *love* their subject, and this love brings the films to life. Not surprisingly, Jacobs has turned his investigations of this form of cinema into another of his own devise. **Urban Peasants** consists of homemovies taken of Jacobs's in-laws when they were children set against a soundtrack of a record teaching Yiddish phrases. The intent of this sound/image dialectic may appear obvious on an immediate presentational level, but ultimately its effect is quite subtle. Here we see those Jews fortunate enough to have been spared the conflagration of the war. They've been fully assimilated by the new culture, yet Yiddish remains, not simply as a reminder of their pasts, but as an alternate source of cultural nourishment. Utilizing these particular homemovies, consequently, isn't an act of quaint nostalgia on Jacobs's part, but rather a deeply serious attempt to come to grips with the problems of time, space, culture, and above all history.

This recontextualization idea figures as well in one of Jacobs's best-known works, **Blonde Cobra**. A bizarre black comedy featuring Jack Smith and Jerry Sims, it was shot by Bob Fleischner around the time of **Star Spangled to Death**. Because of a disagreement among the parties involved as to what direction the film should take, it remained unfinished until Jacobs reshaped it a year or so after if was filmed. The action we see on screen might be likened to out-takes (if such a term were applicable) from **Star Spangled to Death**, consisting as it does of Jack Smith and Jerry Sims playing gangster charades in a cramped kitchen. Guns and knives are brandished in best backyard play-act fashion. The performers constantly peer into or preen before the camera as if it were another character—which in some sense it is. What keeps the film from being a tiresome "beat" fandango is the layering effect Jacobs's editing of the material creates—separating spectator from spectacle. Generous portions of black leader mark off each visual fragment. The soundtrack, meanwhile, is dominated by the voice of Jack Smith telling stories of "Madame Nescience ... dreaming of musty old memories, memories she thought she had forgot ... exuding effluviums from the musty past." Smith being Smith, this is all part of a (muddy) stream of consciousness that includes personal confessions ("A mother's wisdom has dragged me down to this!") and random remarks on life in general ("God is not dead, he is just marvelously sick").

"Jack says I made the film too heavy," Jacobs confessed in a program note, an assessment borne out by **Blonde Cobra**'s critical reputation as some sort of apotheosis of gloom and doom. Yet while different in design from Smith's works, **Blonde Cobra** is at heart—like **Flaming Creatures**—very much a comedy. Smith's narration, which dominates the film, is hilarious. The serious (and in Smith's view "heavy") aspect comes from the visceral impact of the images as they suddenly burst out from the predominant inky blackness of the screen—looming neo-expressionist shadow figures. What we see takes on the aspect of rushes for a newsreel, looming before us like long buried memories of the past—homemovies of the subconscious.

Jacobs's design for **Blonde Cobra** (the title is an amalgam of **Blonde Venus** and **Cobra Woman**) includes instructions for a radio to be turned on at some point during the film's projection. "It hardly ever happens," Jacobs complained in a *Film Culture* interview (#67/68/69, pp. 65-86), "If your film is in focus and on the screen, that seems to be as much as you can ask. I was interested from the beginning in creative projection. I feel it's half the movie-making maybe."

This disposition toward process brings up yet another facet of Jacobs's work—mixed-media performance. Beginning in the mid-Sixties with his

"Apparition Theater of New York" shows, Jacobs put together productions dealing with the most primitive aspects of spectacle. Utilizing slides and sequences from his films, Jacobs and his performers explore the realm of shadow theater—the dramatic form Jacobs finds most crucial to the development of the cinema. 3-D effects play a role in these works as well, though not with the glitz and slickness generally associated with such forms. The multiple-projection techniques Jacobs has devised to create stereoscopic visual effects recall pre-cinematic toys. Yet while returning cinema to its origins, Jacobs's mixed-media spectacles also take things one step further. Like Smith's slide shows and theater pieces, Jacobs's "Apparition Theater" events infuse an increasingly rigidified avant-garde with the healthy air of informality. Jacobs's appeal is plainly directed at the childlike wonder latent within all spectators. These tinkerings, cuttings and pasteings, and holding up of images to light are inextricably tied to a fundamental populism. There are no ivory towers here, only sand castles. Consequently, Jacobs operates at some remove from a system that—thanks to **Tom Tom the Piper's Son**—regards him with respect. Academe may have wrested from its context a work to be celebrated as a classroom classic, but the rest of Jacobs is at heart no more consumable than Smith. His multifariousness serves him well. There is no *one* Ken Jacobs, but many. There is no linearity to his development. It is as if Jacobs were somehow *there* all at once: the bohemian joyousness, the fascination with process, the love of texture, the delight in the commonplace, the respect for the past. The challenge that remains—for us as much as for Jacobs—is to discover another setting for these utopian designs, which is no easy task. A cinema neither vulgar nor snobbish is something of an orphan.

OWEN LAND (GEORGE LANDOW).
Born in New Haven, Connecticut, 1944.

1961—*Two Pieces for the Precarious Life* (8mm, color) (unavailable)
Faulty Pronoun Reference, Comparison, and Punctuation of the Restrictive or Non-Restrictive Element (8mm, color) (unavailable)
A Stringent Prediction at the Early Hermaphroditic Stage (8mm, color) (unavailable)
1963—*Are Era* (16mm, color, 3 min.)
Fleming Faloon (16mm, color, 10 min.)
1964—*Richard Kraft at the Playboy Club* (8mm, color, 8 min.)
Fleming Faloon Screening (8mm, color, 1½ min.)
1965—*The Leopard Skin* (8mm, color, 4 min.)

1965—*Not a Case of Lateral Displacement* (8mm, color,
8 min.)
Adjacent Yes, But Simultaneous (8mm, color, 3 min.)
*This Film Will Be Interrupted after 11 Minutes by a
Commercial* (16mm, color and b&w, 12 min.)
(unavailable)

1966—*Film in Which There Appear Sprocket Holes, Edge
Lettering, Dirt Particles, Etc.* (16mm, color, 4½ min.)
Diploteratology or Bardo Follies (16mm, color,
20 min.)

1968—*The Film That Rises to the Surface of Clarified
Butter* (16mm, b&w, 9½ min.)

1969—*Institutional Quality* (16mm, color, 5 min.)

1971—*Remedial Reading Comprehension* (16mm, color,
7 min.)
What's Wrong with This Picture, Part 1 (16mm,
color and b&w, 7 min.)

1972—*What's Wrong with This Picture, Part 2* (16mm,
color and b&w, 3 min.)

1973—*Thank You Jesus for the Eternal Present, Part 1*
(16mm, color and b&w, 5½ min.)

1974—*Thank You Jesus for the Eternal Present, Part 2:
A Film of Their 1973 Spring Tour Commissioned
by Christian World Liberation Front of Berkeley
California* (16mm, color and b&w, 10 min.)

1976—*New Improved Institutional Quality: In the Envi-
ronment of Liquids and Nasals a Parasitic Vowel
Sometimes Develops* (16mm, color, 5 min.)
Wide Angle Saxon (16mm, color, 22 min.)
No Sir, Orison (16mm, color, 3 min.)

1979—*On the Marriage Broker Joke as Cited by Sigmund
Freud in Wit and Its Relation to the Unconscious,
or Can the Avant-Garde Artist Be Wholed?* (16mm,
color, 17 min.)

Unless otherwise indicated,
the films listed above are available from the
Film-Makers' Cooperative and the Canyon Cinema Cooperative.

This is not an article about George Landow but about his maker. Ordinary distinctions between creator and context blur when a superstructure
interfaces with the figure it is ostensibly designed to support, as it has in
Landow's case. For close to two decades he has remained one of the American avant-garde mainstream's most consistently well-regarded superstars—
comparable in sheer durability to Joan Crawford. This is perfectly understandable in light of Landow's manifest talent and enormous reserve of technical

skill. But what it has meant in critical practice is that, in the final analysis, Landow has yet to be finally analyzed.

Though a recognized film talent since the mid-Sixties, critical attention to Landow didn't begin in earnest until the Seventies, when the style generally associated with his name became established through such films as **Institutional Quality** and **Remedial Reading Comprehension**. Reworking the formal conceits of television commercials and instructional films of the sort shown in U.S. schools during the immediate postwar period (e.g. "How To Be a Good Citizen," "Did This Ever Happen To You?") into networks of puns, allusions, jokes, and visual metaphors, Landow's films quickly found favor with most audiences for their brevity and wit. Like Bruce Conner and Robert Nelson (two filmmakers with whom he has *some* characteristics in common), Landow has functioned in this area as one of the avant-garde's most popular comedy filmmakers. It is his serious side that has received the most attention, however, in recent years, especially in relation to the growing critical consensus against narrativity's alleged threat to all rational thought.

The viewer's inability to follow the instructions of the mock I.Q. test given in **Institutional Quality** ("Write the number 3 on what you would touch," the film's narrator orders) or to identify with the unseen character of Madge in **Remedial Reading Comprehension** ("Suppose your name is Madge and you've just cooked some rice"; "Mmm, this rice is delicious") is seen in this context as not only underscoring the commercial cinema's duplicity, but also moving the spectator toward a new level of consciousness. "Shaken from his previously held position as dreamer," writes Landow enthusiast Vera Dika,* "the viewer is now involved in a consciously opposing function: one which demands directed thought and language formation rather than the self-conscious emotive responses elicited by the classical fiction film." Bracingly original as this new-found spectator status may appear, however, questions immediately arise as to whether Landow's works are truly capable of producing such results.

> *I.Q.* begins with a shot of the back of a girl's head and a rapid cut to her face—as if the screen were a test booklet lying face down and then turned over. A harshly formal voice intones "This is a test of how well you can follow directions." It is not a test of how well you can answer questions or assimilate ideas. Instructions are recited: "Do exactly what I tell you." "Do not ask questions." "Do not guess." "Do not worry." "Do not look at the picture." "Listen carefully to the first problem." These solicit responses which would negate the illusionism in a narrative film, and by their impossibility prophesy future spheres of innovation.†

---

*"*Wide Angle Saxon:* An Examination of the Viewer as Reader," *Film Reader* #3 (1978), p. 222.
†Paul S. Arthur, "The Calesthenics of Vision—Open Instructions on the Films of George Landow," *Artforum*, vol. X, no. 1 (Sept. 1971), p. 74.

The film begins without immediate reference to marriage brokers. Rapturous moans are heard over a close-up of a woman's half-open mouth. At first one supposes the moaning is of sexual origin but this assumption is soon subsequently modified, suggesting that her pleasure is not sexual but religious. The moans merge into a chorale and the preface to a text on mysticism is superimposed over her mouth. The double reading invited by the moaning foreshadows the multiple interpretations of marriage broker anecdotes.*

Two different writers, two different films, yet the thoughts expressed are almost identical. Both analyses in reproducing the work's linearity have been forced into what Christian Metz has called "a mirror reduplication of the film's own ideological inspiration." This is not an uncommon state of affairs in discussions of narrative cinema, but it carries a different connotation in a non-narrative one—especially where liberation from the yoke of ideology is the presumed goal. Simply put, Landow's films are as closed and predetermined in their desired effect as the sort after which they are modelled.

Admittedly, getting a genuine critical grip on Landow is no easy task. In point of fact, the critical contrast method used above is not all that far from the demonstration of different types of rice in **Remedial Reading Comprehension**. Still, some other means of getting outside of Landow in order better to look in must be discovered, for as the situation now stands, even presumed critical disagreements take on the form of utter harmoniousness as in the exchange over **Remedial Reading Comprehension** between Louis Hock and Fred Camper that appeared on the pages of *Film Culture* a few years ago (#52 and #63-64). Camper (as all who speak of Landow tend to) took note of the film's use of "distancing" effects that "make us aware, force us to relate to its abstract structure." Hock, while not entirely denying the truth of Camper's claims, spoke of them as being "nebulous and partial" and advanced the notion that critics need to recognize that Landow's film "vibrates metaphorically." This Hock proceeded to do, working in dutifully linear fashion through the work's compact arrangement of image and sound material (the sleeping woman, the running man, Madge, the rice demonstration, etc.). But rather than provide an original critical insight, Hock is in fact merely following directions on the label indicated by Landow himself: "The important thing to see is that the film contains visual metaphors" (program notes). Together, Hock and Camper produce a "New Improved" **Remedial Reading Comprehension** very much along the lines of Landow's own **New Improved Institutional Quality**—the first of his films to recognize openly the context such critical devotion had created for him.

---

*Sue Ann Estevez, "George Landow's Marriage Broker Joke," *Millennium Film Journal* #10/11 (Fall/Winter 1981-82), p. 200.

Utilizing the better part of the soundtrack narration of the first film, this remake (subtitled *In the Environment of Liquids and Nasals a Parasitic Vowel Sometimes Develops*) places an actor within a complete three-dimensional set of the living room test illustration (which appeared in the original as a flat photograph). This actor proceeds to number items as before, responding to the commands of the narrator. Towards the conclusion of **New Improved**, however, instead of the images seen in the first film, references to other Landow works crop up. The running man of **Remedial Reading Comprehension** appears not in a shot from that film, but rather by means of a crude parody reproduction in which a sign bearing the words "This is a film about you" (superimposed over his image in the original) hangs from a rope around his neck. Another parody follows in a similarly staged form, reproducing the color test pattern woman of Landow's **Film in Which There Appear Sprocket Holes, Edge Lettering, Dirt Particles, Etc.** That early Landow work was made from a piece of commercial footage showing a woman's head and shoulders bordered by colored squares. Landow reprinted it in a manner that made the visual characteristics mentioned in the title appear prominently. Produced prior to the emergence of the structural sub-genre, when pure textual fascination appeared to be Landow's chief delight (e.g. **Fleming Faloon, Bardo Follies**), **Film in Which ..., Etc.** was later seen purely in structural terms. "The initial task is one of orientation, the selection of a point of reference, a coordinate from which one can correctly 'read' the temporal reality of the film," wrote Paul Arthur of this Landow effort. Consequently, its parody appearance in **New Improved Institutional Quality** (as a "parasitic vowel"?) is indicative of a willingness on Landow's part to confront that which has been made of him, a willingness not without a decided sense of ambivalence.

Arthur's invocation of the concept of the "correct" reading is crucial to Landow—though not in the way that Arthur would appear to believe. In narrative films "correct" readings are produced largely by means of downplaying the artistic processes that avant-garde films foreground. The "correct" reading would here constitute a recognition of such processes. The problem with Landow, however, is that such a reading does not necessarily preclude the establishment of an effect ideologically equivalent to that of a narrative, i.e. a message. This has become especially apparent in recent years with Landow's conversion to fundamentalist Christianity, which produced a radical change in the substance, though not the style, of his work. The threat of an "incorrect" reading now haunts him.

Wide Angle Saxon, for example, contains a parody of Hollis Frampton's **Nostalgia** entitled *Regrettable Redding Condescension*. This film-within-a-film is credited to one "Al Rutcurts"—"structural" spelled backwards. "People have associated me with Hollis Frampton as if we were some sort of team, which is kind of ridiculous," Landow complained in a *Film Culture* interview (#67-68-69). He also spoke of his conversion. "It is embarrassing even to say that you're a Christian," Landow confessed, "It's not impressive." Pointing out that both Christianity and avant-garde art are "anticonventional" as they have both "broken the rules," Landow did admit to some difficulty as "Christianity has become a convention, and so has avant-garde art in museums. Both have become academicized." The problem therefore is how Landow can make his new-found Christianity count in a context all too willing to subsume it as a mere reference point—like the eastern mysticism that previously served as a Landow preoccupation. **Wide Angle Saxon** shows Landow to be keenly aware of this fact. As we are told by a TV-type announcer who sits behind a desk in a wood-paneled office, the film's nominal hero "Earl Greaves" has had a religious conversion experience in which he surrendered all his worldly possessions. "The actual moment of conviction comes to him while he is watching an experimental film at the Walker Arts Center." As might be expected with Landow, none of this is shown directly (despite the announcer's "Well here, let me show you... "). We see images of the film (the Frampton parody) and a man (presumably Earl Greaves) clapping in a shot designed to suggest an audience and an auditorium surrounding him. The conversion is evoked through the announcer's efforts to underscore the meaning of the word "sin" seen as a parallel to a bit of television news footage in which a reporter repeatedly stumbles over the name of a Latin American dictator—"sin" as error.

"I had to consider the Bible," Landow explained in the *Film Culture* interview, "as either a true book or a false book. I couldn't accept that it could be either partly true or partly false." In much the same spirit, therefore, Landow's recent films must either be dealt with as wholly Christian or not at all—any other consideration constitutes an "incorrect" reading. Landow would appear to be doubtful that they can get such a reading, to judge from the evidence provided in his film **On the Marriage Broker Joke as Cited by Sigmund Freud in Wit and Its Relation to the Unconscious, or Can the Avant-Garde Artist Be Wholed?** In it yet another announcer figure speaks of a religious interpretation of the joke in which the marriage broker is God, the suitor Christ, and the prospective bride "fallen humanity, undeserving of the redemption which Christ offers through the grace of God." This announcer then refers to a counter interpretation in which the marriage broker is a panderer and the bride a prostitute (Christ, presumably, is still the suitor). He then cites the "textual corruption" that in some versions of this tale has made "panderer" into "panda." Landow's film is then off and running in a thoroughly wacky style with two giant pandas (men in panda suits) taking over the action in order to make a "structural film," a category they liken to when engineers design an airplane or bridge: "they build a model to find out if it will fall apart too soon. The film shows where all the stresses are." The stresses in this instance have to do with the panda filmmaker's ostensible subject, "Japanese salted plums, among other things."

*On the Marriage Broker Joke as
Cited by Sigmund Freud in Wit
and Its Relation to the
Unconscious, or Can the
Avant-Garde Artist Be Wholed?*
by Owen Land (George
Landow). Still courtesy The
American Federation of
Arts/Film Department.

But to go off in a direction that would analyze such a diegesis would
risk surrender to the repetitive patterns of past critiques. Better—and simpler—to skip to the end, where the message is. There we find "the heavenly
sweetness of Christ's excellent love" referred to much in the spirit of "a
word from our sponsor." The problem is whether anyone in the avant-garde
context is willing to buy it. Landow's *Film Culture* interviewer, P. Gregory
Springer, mentions, in passing reference to Landow's Christianity, religion's
"unfashionableness" in an avant-garde where "there is a spiritual tradition

*On the Marriage
Broker Joke ....*

but it is not really a Christian tradition." This is surely one of the understate-
ments of the century in light of Kenneth Anger, Harry Smith, et al. Fundamentalist complaints about the influence of "secular humanism" pale by
comparison.

Where Landow can go next in relation to this is uncertain. But it is
perhaps significant that shortly after the release of **On the Marriage Broker
Joke** he changed his name to Owen Land.

Owen Land has expressed an interest in working in video.

BRUCE CONNER.
Born in McPherson, Kansas, 1933.

1958—*A Movie* (16mm, b&w, 12 min.)
1961—*Cosmic Ray* (16mm, b&w, 4 min.)
1964—*Vivian* (16mm, b&w, 3 min.)
1965—*Ten Second Film* (16mm, b&w, 10 sec., silent)
      Report (16mm, b&w, 13 min.)
1967—*Looking for Mushrooms* (8mm, color, 3 min.)
      The White Rose (8mm, b&w, 7 min.)
      Breakaway (16mm, b&w, 5 min.)
      Liberty Crown (16mm, b&w, 5 min.)
1969—*Permian Strata* (16mm, b&w, 4 min.)
1973—*Marilyn Times Five* (16mm, b&w, 13 min.)
1975—*Crossroads* (16mm, b&w, 36 min.)
      Take the 5:10 to Dreamland (16mm; b&w and
      sepia; 5 min., 10 sec.)
1977—*Valse Triste* (16mm; b&w and sepia; 5 min., 5 sec.)
1978—*Mongoloid* (16mm, b&w, 4 min.)
1982—*America Is Waiting* (16mm; b&w; 3 min., 5 sec.)
in progress: The Soul Stirrers: By and By

Bruce Conner's films are available from the
Film-Makers' Cooperative and the Canyon Cinema Cooperative.
Looking for Mushrooms and *The White Rose* are also available in 16mm.

Of all American avant-garde filmmakers, Bruce Conner is unquestionably the least controversial. After a brief initial coolness to his work, Conner
quickly found favor with both critics and audiences in a manner that has
continued to this day. Few movie viewers have had any difficulty in com-
prehending either the meaning or the methodology of such collage classics
as **A Movie** or **Cosmic Ray**. Their wild mixtures of newsreels, commercials,
cartoons, and "blue" movies fit neatly within the context of postwar American "black" humor (Lenny Bruce, Terry Southern, William Burroughs, etc.).
"Pop Art" has likewise provided an associative link, matching up Conner's
use of television ad images with the celebrations of Madison Avenue banality
in the paintings of Warhol, Rosenquist, and Lichtenstein. In more recent times

rock video has served as a Conner touchstone, both stylistically (**Vivian** and **Breakaway**—the latter starring future rock video fave Toni Basil—are clear forerunners of the form) and contextually, as MTV's ad logos frequently make use of the same genre of "found" visual materials (newsreels, industrial films, instructional shorts, etc.) that so fascinate Conner.

As might be expected, this brand of cultural familiarity hasn't set too well with an avant-establishment intent on taking Conner "seriously" at all costs. Scott Cook, in an article in *Millennium Film Journal* (#7/8/9, Fall/Winter 1980-81), compares Conner to the Cubists. Ken Kelman in *Film Culture** has claimed to have discovered links between Conner and Stan Brakhage. Though admitting that "there appears little enough in common between their actual films," Kelman insists that the two constitute the "clearest example" of the "master-apprentice relationship" in the avant-garde today. (No points for guessing who is master and who is apprentice.) In Kelman's eyes, Brakhage and Conner both produce works that are "emphatically cinemagistic as opposed to literary or dramatic" and are thus one and the same, a harsh reminder to those viewers so presumptuous as to see narrative elements in Conner. It is all obviously in their Hollywood-clouded imaginations.

At a screening of a number of his works at New York's "Collective for Living Cinema" in the spring of 1984, Conner himself cited a far less lofty source of inspiration for his work—the Marx Brothers film **Duck Soup**. In the climax of that 1933 classic, the four brothers (and Groucho's much put-upon *inamorata* Margaret Dumont) find themselves in a small farm house with a war raging around them on all sides. Groucho gives Harpo orders to get help. Harpo places a "Help Wanted" sign outside the door. At this point a montage sequence ensues in which armies of men, tanks, cars, airplanes, and even herds of jungle beasts are seen rampaging to the rescue. Conner pays clear hommage to this sequence in an early segment of **A Movie** in which Indians pursuing a wagon train are joined by race cars and herds of elephants. On the soundtrack during this sequence a jaunty passage from Respighi's "The Pines of Rome" can be heard. But as the sound of a dissonant trumpet breaks through the score, slapstick gaiety gives way to horror. Race cars are seen crashing on a track with bodies flying through the air. An early Thirties roadster takes a nose dive off a high cliff as the music comes to a brief, abrupt pause and the words "The End" appear on the screen. This does not signify the actual end of **A Movie**, however. The film picks itself up again immediately afterward, providing (with continuing Respighi accompaniment) images of disaster (the Hindenberg crash), danger (a high wire act performing over city streets far below), and misery (plague victims, dead animals). It all finally comes to an oddly unsettling conclusion

---

*"Portrait of the Young Man as Artist: From the Notebooks of Robert Beavers," *Film Culture* #67/68/69 (1979), p. 195.

with the image of a diver going underwater followed by a shot of sunlight twinkling on the ocean's surface. It is as if mankind, having failed, has elected to return to the sea from whence it came.

The intrusion of "The End" after the car crash scene isn't the first in the film. **A Movie**'s opening moments are taken up by a number of "false starts"—images that begin to unwind only to halt abruptly with "The End."

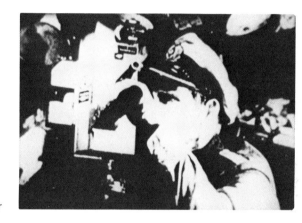

A Movie, by Bruce Conner

A Movie, by Bruce Conner

First Conner's name holds the screen for a relatively inordinate length of time. A bit of academy leader follows, counting down from 10 to 3, a shot of a woman taking her stockings off appears, and then "The End." A more elaborate "false start" soon follows with a shot of a submarine captain looking through a periscope. We next see a woman in underclothes suggestively reclining on a bed. Evidently horrified by this sight, the captain hastily barks (unheard) orders to his crew. A torpedo shell is seen speeding through the water, followed by a shot of an atomic explosion. The "The End" that follows evokes something more than the inevitable consequence of such a head-on collision between fear and desire. It is as if the movie itself were a conscious entity, willing images into being, offering them up to us, and then snatching them away.

The notion of a film's having "a life of its own" is scarcely a new one (e.g. Chuck Jones's classic cartoon **Duck Amuck** covering much of the same pull-the-rug-out-from-under-you territory in 1953), but Conner places it in a new dimension. The means by which montage gets us from one place to another are seen in terms of a logic of which the filmmaker is not master, but servant. A shot of Indians high on a cliff automatically leads to a pursuit, as it has in countless westerns. The process brings to mind Christian Metz's oft-remarked-upon error in his early semiotic studies (*Essais sur la significa- tion au cinema*, Tome II) in seeing such an image as connoting "the idea of menace or danger" in and of itself—ignoring the cultural conditioning that would regard native Americans in such a reflexively racist way. It is this same cultural conditioning that most concerns Conner, who, by placing one brand of chase on top of another (i.e. the race cars, the elephant stampede), undoes the work of the original. This process strikes at the heart of Conner's method of direct intervention in the representational status quo. Understanding that each image he deals with has an already predetermined purpose and definition, Conner sets about bending that image in another direction, through context alteration. The old meaning is unseated, but no new meaning is imposed with the same degree of force, for Conner's alter- ation leaves the first meaning's trace behind.

This process can best be seen in Conner's most ambitious film, **Report**, a study of the Kennedy assassination—or rather, to be more precise, a study of the *images* of the Kennedy assassination, for as Conner shows this signal public tragedy, it was by and large a matter of images. In the opening of Conner's film we see Kennedy and his wife riding in an open limousine in the Dallas procession just moments prior to the shooting. As if on a mechanized loop the same shot runs by over and over again as we hear the voice of an announcer describing the scene. As the car carrying the Kennedys passes out of view, the fatal shots ring out, the word "finish" (from a bit of academy leader off the end of a projection reel) hits the screen. Now totally white, the screen begins to flash strobe-like while the announcer reports the details of what has just transpired as he learns of them. With the official announcement of Kennedy's death read out, academy leader counting down from 10 to 3 runs by several times in silence. The next image we see, also silent, is of a picador in a bullfighting arena. The announcer's voice returns, now describing events that took place earlier in the day—the arrival of Kennedy's plane at the Dallas airport. Conner makes full use of the "sick" comic possibilities of this speech, juxtaposing a description of the "gun-metal gray limousine" with a shot of the rifle (allegedly) used in the assassination held aloft by police officers. It passes across the screen several times in the same "loop" fashion as the limousine seen earlier. The film's final segment is devoted to similar audiovisual foreshadowings, some direct (the announcer speaks of the parade route while on screen we see the Kennedy funeral cortege) and some allusive (the picador and bullfight imagery is a play on Hemingway's "Death in the Afternoon," a title the press frequently invoked in descriptions of the assassination). Conner's montage ideas become bolder still as commercials for refrigerators and office equipment and shots of the climactic sequence of **The Bride of Frankenstein** wend their way into a text that quickly includes more funeral footage and the assassination of accused assassin Lee Harvey Oswald. Conner's attitude to all of this is plain. Television presents the assassination to us much as it would any well-planned "special." The act therefore takes the form of a kind of mass ritual sacrifice— the by-product of industrial capitalism's *soi distant* blood lust. This all becomes abundantly clear in **Report**'s grand finale. As the announcer's voice details directions for the route Kennedy's limousine will take, we see a secretary in an office (a commercial image) intercut with a shot of the ceremony inaugurating Kennedy as president. The secretary leans over her console and presses a small button with the word "sell" printed on it as the screen fades to black.

Made only two years after the assassination, **Report** initially disturbed many viewers. But as Conner noted in his "Collective" talk, time has a way of changing all that. The film seems less outrageous today. Conner is fully aware of this process and has used it in his work, not simply to underscore shifts in social surface effects (changes in dress style, mannerisms, etc.) but on a more fundamental level.

Conner's **Crossroads** is constructed entirely out of the most highly charged image of our time—the explosion of the atomic bomb. Thirty-six minutes in length, the film shows us the detonation of a low-level device at Bikini Atoll in the late Forties over and over again from every angle. Though weapons infinitely more powerful have been developed since then, it is this image that has remained with us culturally as "the bomb." We have seen it countless times already in newsreels and on television. It is the bomb featured in the finale of Kubrick's **Dr. Strangelove**. It is the bomb that blows up the stripper in Conner's own **A Movie**. Now we look at it again (and again and again) and by doing so take the first step toward dealing with it as pure phenomenon. After the first few blasts, connotations of horror inevitably give way to fascination—helped in large measure by the tinkling Terry Riley score used in the film's second half. Yet in teaching us to "stop worrying and love the bomb" in a way Kubrick never could, Conner doesn't simply turn the apocalypse into a "head" movie—repetition underscores the loss of affectivity every image is heir to. We have been inured to horror before—as in Vietnam, where constant television exposure turned it all into one nonstop atrocity exhibit.

Loss of affectivity has made its presence known in Conner's work in other unforeseen ways as well. **Mongoloid** and **America Is Waiting** are both satires in the tradition of **A Movie**—with education the target of the first, and jingoism of the second. But their impact is considerably lessened by the fact that both partake of the image repertoire of post-punk trendiness associated with the "new wave" music (Devo, David Byrne, and Brian Eno) on their soundtracks. Admittedly, this situation has arisen as a result of forces quite outside of Conner's hands. As a collage filmmaker he was from the very outset compelled to draw on images within the public domain—the cultural refuse of another time, principally promotional materials and documentary footage of the postwar era. These same images have in recent years gained currency as chic artifacts—condescendingly embraced for their quaintness in a way that might be described as "softcore camp." The points Conner wishes to make about conformity and militarism consequently become blurred by the images' newly won status as objects of thrift-shop style consumption.

Conner has met with more success in two other works utilizing similar footage, **Take the 5:10 to Dreamland** and **Valse Triste**. Both are tinted a rich faded-photo-album brown. Both have non-rock scores (Patrick Gleeson and Jean Sibelius, respectively). Their montage strategy, rather than linking one shot to the next with firm severity, regards each as a discrete event. In **Take the 5:10 to Dreamland** shots of rain on suburban streets, a girl bending over to tie a bowling shoe, a child at play, and a bland suburban interior take on a tone of eerie calm tinged with nostalgia. **Valse Triste** links things up to some degree; its shots of Kansas in the Forties, trains pulling into yards, and a boy sleeping in bed suggest a childhood recollection of Conner's. But suggest is all it does. In Conner's other collage works each shot's initial meaning (the one existing prior to the moment Conner got his hands on it) gave way to the new context the filmmaker created for it. In this diptych, however, the initial context is not retracted so severely. Nothing new is deliberately applied. Each image seems to float on a sea of possible associations, never truly coming down on the side of a definitive one—save for that implied by the film's overall context of nostalgia. We look at the past from the outside. The film does not recall it, so much as it re-presents it—like a fly in amber. We thus see a world so different from our own that it could be that of another planet. Bathed in calm (very much like the shots of the crossroads that conclude Antonioni's **Eclipse**) these images beckon to us, but remain at arm's length.

Conner's obsession with the past will doubtless take yet another turn with his new project currently in progress, a documentary feature on the life and times of the legendary gospel group the Soul Stirrers. **The Soul Stirrers: By and By** (Conner's working title) will consist of both archival material of the group and new interview and concert footage. Conner has made films utilizing images of his own making before (**Vivian, Breakaway,** and **Liberty Crown** being the most noteworthy), but their rapid fire visual style isn't likely to play too significant a role in a film that will examine this group's history at close range, touching on its effect on other forms of black music, particularly as its most famous member, the late Sam Cooke, left the group to become one of pop music's most influential stars.

This is not to say that Conner intends to abandon his filmmaking past entirely in this new work. He plans to use his usual montage methods in several sequences of the film, such as one in which archive footage of Soul Stirrers founder R. H. Harris singing is intercut with shots of birds. The idea behind the sequence comes from Harris's claim that nature is his chief source of vocal inspiration. Whether such bits will stand as self-enclosed *grande syntagmatiques* or will be woven into a larger overall structure markedly different from the sort of straightforward documentary the film at this point appears to suggest, remains to be seen.

The departure Conner is undertaking in making such a film is, of course, more than an aesthetic one. He is leaving the cocoon of the avant-garde for the less certain confines of the commercial marketplace—formally facing off against the horrors his generation of filmmakers has always claimed to find there. This is not Conner's first brush with commerce. He provided technical advice on sequences of **Easy Rider** and **The Last Movie**, both directed by his friend Dennis Hopper. But **The Soul Stirrers: By and By** is far more modestly designed than those Sixties epics. Conner hopes his film will get exposure both on public television and in certain "art" theater situations. What this may all mean in the long run is impossible to surmise at this point. To work with images in the public domain is one thing. Actively to bring oneself into that same domain is another. Conner's new project, by its very nature, may yet win for him the controversy he has managed to elude for so long.

 DAVID BROOKS.
Born in New York City, 1945; Died 1969.

1963—*Jerry* (16mm, color, 3 min., silent)
1964—*Nightspring Daystar* (16mm, color, 18 min.)
1966—*Winter* (16mm, color, 1000 sec.)
1967—*Letter to D. H. in Paris* (16mm, color, 4 min.)
1968—*The Wind Is Driving Him Toward the Open Sea* (16mm, color, 52 min.)
     Eel Creek (16mm, color, 7 min.)
1969—*Carolyn and Me* (16mm, color, 104½ min., unfinished)
David Brooks's films are available from the Film-Makers' Cooperative.

The camera, apparently hand-held, is close to ground level. Aimed at a small, nondescript wooden building (evidently a restaurant or cafe), it suddenly begins to pan to the right. A deserted parking lot and dock area with boats moored nearby come into view as the pan continues its course, eventually making two complete 360° revolutions about the scene. A few people are standing about the dock area. The wind blows in from across the water. A Land Rover pulls into the lot and parks as the camera's movement finally comes to a halt. The shot that follows, taken from a static standing position, is of a man seated on the lot's blacktop surface with a camera in his lap. Peering into its lens, he pivots about in place on the ground several times—executing the very camera movement we saw earlier.

No, this isn't a sequence from a new film by Michael Snow, but an old one by David Brooks, **The Wind Is Driving Him Toward the Open Sea**. Viewed today it appears almost a parody-before-the-fact of **La Region centrale** (which was made in 1971). At the time of its making, however, **The Wind** had no structural cache. It was simply one part of a free and easy mixture of personal diary and *cinéma vérité* documentary, dramatic fragment and visual arabesque. It would be tempting to argue from this and other pieces of cinematic evidence that Brooks was a filmmaker "ahead of his time." To do so, however, would be to miss the point—to see a bit of offhand visual japery as a central figure of style, to pay lip service to the myth of progress that has so damaged the cultural atmosphere of the past decade.

It is an increasingly common practice to place certain figures (e.g. Eisenstein, Vertov, Dreyer) in that category of cultural irreproachability known as the "modern." A massive compendium of judgmental notions, some related to reasoned evaluation, others having more to do with mere snobbishness and faddism, the "modern" has been used on countless occasions to separate—often arbitrarily—the "then" from the "now." In light of the present climate of near-hysterical aesthetic consumerism, the concept is in special need of reconsideration. With Laurie Anderson today and Piña Bausch tomorrow, novelty value quickly subsumes measured estimation as one heralded "innovation" (often little more than a cheap thrill) quickly follows another. Genuine talents of less obvious outward appearance are likely as not to get bypassed in the rush—which brings us back to Brooks and an additional reason why past/present divisions are so misleading in dealing with his work.

David Brooks died in an automobile accident in 1969 at the age of 24 with only six completed works to his credit. There is a well-established mode of discourse reserved for filmmakers cut down in their prime; praise for what was is balanced by mourning for what might have been. This may appear at first an appropriate response, and to some degree it is. The only problem is the way in which it places the filmmaker in a kind of artistic limbo. Rather than enjoying continued validity, achievements sit frozen in a state not quite part of yet not quite removed from history. Alongside it stand a clutch of aesthetic possibilities—a nether region of unfinished "dream" projects, unmade masterpieces. With Brooks the situation is doubly difficult, for unlike a Jean Vigo or Ron Rice he received little attention in his own lifetime. To bring up his name is to start from scratch, as it were, only to come up against the unavoidable inscription death has left on his career.

J. J. Murphy, in his brief study of Brooks published in 1983 in *Film Culture* (#70-71), touches on these areas in describing him as a figure "eclipsed by his early death" and by "the cooler more controlled sensibility of structural film" that followed. To Murphy, Brooks was "one of the most prominent lyricists of the experimental cinema," whose works, particularly **The Wind**, were part of a Sixties-era trend toward "plotless narrative" (e.g. **Pull My Daisy**, **The Flower Thief**, **Senseless**) that Jonas Mekas had cited as "an important aesthetic advance." Seen in this light, Brooks appears as something on the order of an innocent bystander before the onrush of avant-garde film culture's manifest destiny—one stylistic movement ("structural film") smoothly usurping another ("plotless narrative") with the followers of the latter left on the backwash of history. The truth behind this vast oversimplification—inextricably tied to the nature of Brooks's real relation to the various cultural forces surrounding him—is considerably more complex.

> I was born karem Kari Beg in 1889 to a tribe of Kazaks on the plains of Lower Mongolia, was raised on koumiss and kief until the age of three when I was kidnapped by an Arab band and taken to Turkey for sale as a slave. After eight years as houseboy to an Arab chieftan, I escaped to Basutoland, where I lived in a cave and roamed among the beasts. In 1938, when Auguste Villagny came to Africa to film *The Jimmy Walker Story*, I attached myself to the crew as signal-line feed adjustor. After a number of years prospecting in New Guinea, I recently came to America.

So ran an autobiography of Brooks printed in a program note. A typical bit of post-"beat" effrontery, it bears witness to one of the many different strains of influence that circulated about him. Stan Brakhage and Jonas Mekas—to whom Brooks dedicated **Nightspring Daystar**—were both crucial. From the former's obsession with perceptual processes came Brooks's fascination with light and color. From the latter's diary filmmaking style came the joy Brooks took in the commonplace, the everyday event. Gregory Markopoulos—a filmmaker coming from an entirely different aesthetic direction—left his mark as well, particularly in regard to narrative. For just as Markopoulos's **Twice a Man** (1963) assumes the form of a tale fragmented so that all that remains are key interchanges between theme and character, so Brooks, particularly in **Winter** and **The Wind Is Driving Him Toward the Open Sea**, constructs *potential* narratives—films whose arrangements of image and sound continually rub up against the edge of drama.

"All my films begin with breaking up with a girl friend," Brooks once declared in an interview,* a phantom scenario that rises to the surface with periodic insistence in many of his works. In **Winter**, for example, one scene/shot has the camera looking out the window of a moving car as it hurdles down a stretch of highway. Marvin Gaye's "Ain't That Peculiar" rises on the soundtrack (as if coming from the car's radio) and then falls as the image fades out before moving on to another locale. The precise sense of this fragment is difficult to pin down. It is a subjective vision, but whose is unclear. The overall form of **Winter**, as it does not feature on-screen figures who could be called characters in the accepted sense of the term, suggests a pure diary film, a first person vision. Yet the dramatic bracketing that Brooks contrives for this and other shots in the film (synchronized image and sound heavily marked by a fade out at the scene's conclusion) suggests that the "person" involved is not necessarily Brooks himself. This lack of definition haunts the entire structure of the work filled with city and country vistas that loom up on the screen, much in the manner of "establishing shots" in a conventional drama. The whole question of "who is speaking" is, consequently, always involved, which of course is part of the point. We are never sure, for Brooks is never sure either. In itself this constitutes a decisive break with the practice of his avant-garde peers, whose images were always regarded as utterly subjective and absolutely equivalent only to the filmmaker's state of consciousness (Brakhage being the *locus classicus*). But this is not the only thing that sets Brooks in a place apart.

"I had a whole series of personal crises," Brooks recalled in the interview. "In the midst of that I started getting very hung up on my room." In light of what he eventually produced from this situation, this remark is something of an understatement. The image of Brooks's room (seen in the accompanying still) appears in nearly all the films, growing from what he first thought of as "a little movie ... two minutes long," into a constant point of reference, never meaning the same thing twice. On one level this obsession dovetails into Brooks's Brakhage legacy—ordinary possessions transformed by the camera eye into icons of the self. But because of the affective uncertainty Brooks strove to create, it never remains on that level. The room gets its fullest workout in **Winter**, looming up as a refuge for the filmmaker/character. In **Letter to D. H. in Paris** and **The Wind Is Driving Him Toward the Open Sea** it becomes a kind of signature object—like gray felt hats in Melville's films or doves in Franju's. It further stands as a reminder that no image or sound in the film that surrounds it is grounded in a single level of meaning.

---

*"Making Art: An Interview with David Brooks," by Albert Shapiro, *King's Crown Essays*, vol. XIV, no. 1, Spring 1967.

An image seen in several Brooks films, including *Winter* and *The Wind Is Driving Him Toward the Open Sea.* Still courtesy Anthology Film Archives.

In the interview, made while **The Wind Is Driving Him Toward the Open Sea** was still in progress, Brooks spoke of his ideas in relatively conventional story terms. "He comes down from the mountain and goes and finds a boat by the water, swims out to it, and takes it out.... Overnight the boat turns into a big sailboat and he takes it to Nantucket Island. He meets a girl there.... I don't know what's going to happen then...." This uncertainty, coupled with the visceral vigor suggested by Brooks's description of the action, is everywhere apparent in the finished film, but in a radically different—decidedly non-linear—form. The "he" Brooks mentions, for example, is divided up in several ways. On one level the character comes into play in the free-floating subjective shots common to all Brooks films. Then, there's an on-screen character, an unidentified youth played by Jeff Siggins, apparently on some journey to some place or another. Where he is going and why are never discovered—he has no dialogue. The film's other major character, a man named Chandler Moore, is put into sharper personal focus—though he remains off-screen throughout the action. A documentary crew interviews various people in and around Martha's Vineyard about Chandler, a mysterious but apparently well-respected loner whose erratic behavior, climaxed by his recent disappearance, may have come as a direct result of his war experiences and an inability to adjust to civilian life.

It would be a fairly simple matter to tie these three areas together in some relatively straightforward fashion. The subjective shots could be related to either Chandler or the youth. The latter, for example, could be Chandler's son searching for his long-lost father. But Brooks refuses to take this easy way out, choosing instead to add further elements to the stew, including what might be likened to the film's sole female character. Periodically newspaper clippings blaze across the screen telling the story of "the loneliest little girl in the world," the "Kumari"—living goddess of a religious cult in Nepal. Kept in strict isolation throughout childhood, she is replaced on reaching puberty by the election of yet another living goddess to "Kumari" status.

"The object of any man's exploration must ultimately be a woman, a Kumari," Brooks explained in a program note for the film. But by fracturing his story into pieces, Brooks places this otherwise standard operational narrative motor in crisis. What would normally be a search performed by characters becomes instead a search demanded of the movie viewer, deprived of clearly stated links between the shots, the youth, Chandler Moore, and the "Kumari." The very existence of the possibility of links may not be apparent until well into the progress of the film.

A clue, of sorts, is provided by the scenes that open and close **The Wind**. In the first, a group of philosophy professors (including future film commentator Stanley Cavell) are seen standing in a field arguing over the ways of proving the "reality of grass," inspired by a passing remark from one of them about the joy of seeing Joe DiMaggio hit a homerun. In the closing scene, two couples (boy/girl, boy/girl) romp about in a field (perhaps the same one in which the philosophers stood) in some sort of improvised celebratory dance. Between a moment of intellectual inquiry and a moment of romantic free expression stands a search for identity. It is neither inspired by the first moment nor resolved by the second. They simply indicate a field of possible inquiry.

"In the film a boy travels, while we search for a man, Chandler Moore," Brooks has explained. "He is never found, but we see the world he has made for himself." Hardly an unprecedented situation. A search like all narrative searches, **The Wind** hovers around the identity process of the male—white and heterosexual as in all such searches. But there is no John Wayne to be found at the end of all this—or Joe DiMaggio either. Rather, we must chart a course across a series of what might be called audiovisual relays (the youth, Chandler Moore, the "Kumari" all serving as touchstone figures) deprived of any definitive shape. No cues or presentational methods commonly associated with deconstructive processes crop up along the way. We're on our own.

That few films in the structural sub-genre that came in Brooks's wake offered such audiovisual informality doesn't preclude its removal from the filmmaking scene. For while the "structural" dominated the avant-establishment's consciousness, interest in the "plotless narrative" continued to expand on several filmmaking fronts throughout the Seventies.

1968, the year **The Wind Is Driving Him Toward the Open Sea** was released, saw the production of Godard's **One Plus One** and Straub and Huillet's **Der Bräutigam, die Komödiantin und der Zuhälter/The Bridegroom the Actress and the Pimp,** two collage works whose unorthodox mixtures of diverse cultural strands (the Rolling Stones, pulp fiction, and revolutionary rhetoric for Godard, a Bruckner play and the poetry of Juan de la Cruz for Straub-Huillet) went on to figure in the style of many of their creators' subsequent works—such "plotless narratives" as **Passion,** and **Dalla Nube alla Resistenza/From the Cloud to the Resistance.** The late Seventies also saw Yvonne Rainer's transition from dance theater choreographer to filmmaker with such "plotless narrative" moral/cultural meditations as **Kristina Talking Pictures** and **Journeys from Berlin/1971.** The work of Curt McDowell, coming to a prominence of sorts around the same time, was similarly structured, taking narrative plotlessness into new uncharted regions in **Taboo: The Single and the LP** (discussed at length in the section of this book devoted to his work). Recently, new breakthroughs in the form have come from Alexander Kluge in his **Die Macht der Gefühle/The Power of Emotions,** a visual essay on the affectivity of opera and its relation to history and the social order which freely mixes documentary sequences with brief dramatic sketches.

It would be a mistake to view this stylistic tendency in terms of an organized movement or to claim any degree of direct influence by Brooks on the filmmaking practices of any of the parties mentioned above. But it would be no less of an error to dismiss, as Murphy does in the passage quoted earlier, "plotless narrative" as the concern of one era alone. In addition to Frank and Leslie and Ron Rice (the filmmakers Murphy cites) mention must also be made (again) of the contributions of Jack Smith and Ken Jacobs to the overall loosening of filmmaking constraints. In the same spirit the works of such cinematic mavericks as Jean-Daniel Pollet (**Méditerranée, Le Horla**) and Marcel Hanoun (**Octobre à Madrid, Le Printemps**) must be acknowledged for their contribution to the altering of narrative design.

What is characteristic of these, and countless other innovative instances is the spectacle of a filmmaker consciously seeking to ride the edge—neither embracing narrative principles nor entirely avoiding them, never reducing audiovisual elements to a single common denominator. Seeking to avoid narrative "illusionism," the "structural" has, often as not, replaced it with a phenomenological schematic in which the spectator's perceptual consciousness is wedded to the spectacle before him in a far more absolute (and consequently mystificatory) way than that of the most conventional of narrative films. Even so vaunted a "structural" talent as Snow sought relief in the looser design of his **"Rameau's Nephew" by Diderot (Thanx to Dennis**

Young) by Wilma Schoen. What has always, and will continue to be, available to filmmakers are alternatives to conventions of every kind. Whether a convenient label or name-tag for the recent innovations of Godard, Straub-Huillet, Rainer, Kluge, and many others presents itself is of little concern. What is clear is that Brooks's work belongs in this filmmaking front line. The only thing keeping him outside of it is the conventions of critical perception. Dead artists are supposed to speak to us with the calm voice of the Master—not the active, unsettled one of films like **Winter**, **The Wind**, and **Eel Creek**. That Brooks's films are as fresh now as the day they were made is a fact that must be faced. There is no point in speculating on what road he might have taken (the rushes that constitute the unfinished **Carolyn and Me** are no more revealing of their creator's ultimate intentions than those of Eisenstein's **Que Viva Mexico**). There is considerable reason to believe, however, that, had he continued, his work would have profited from the aesthetic atmosphere just outlined. It is for this reason that David Brooks cannot be said to be exactly "of" his time or "ahead" of it. Brooks is plainly and simply *there*—on the line, with all filmmakers—now and for some considerable time to come.

. . . the argument thus far

The filmmakers dealt with in the preceding section are all part of a postwar American context that has almost invariably been utilized as a focal point for discussions of avant-garde and independent work in general. In one sense this is most appropriate. The quality of the films in question and the astonishing vigor of that moviemaking movement were practically without precedent. Nevertheless, beneath this surface dazzle, the fact that the context itself is largely the result of the unceasing publicity efforts of a number of critics and commentators (Jonas Mekas, Annette Michelson, et al.) cannot be ignored. Mixing sincere sentiment with inane hyperbole this scholarly/journalistic ménage did manage to bring deserved attention to any number of worthwhile talents. At the same time, however, it brought about the far less justifiable impression of an imaginary union of filmmakers of wildly divergent means and ends. This figure of rhetorical fancy (Brakhagemarkopoulosangerjacobsgehrframptonetc.) has constantly been depicted in heroic terms, leaping from one artistic triumph to another, untroubled by problems attendant upon mere mortal filmmakers. Offering itself up as the last word in cinematic experience (without providing so much as the first word about the far more complex whys and wherefores of its actual highly troubled history), this cultural monolith has served to block from view every form of avant-garde and independent endeavor with which it doesn't happen to be on a first-name basis.

The most vociferous attacks on this construct have been lodged by British writer/filmmaker Peter Gidal, in whose view it constitutes nothing less than an attempt to "imperialize artistic production in line with North America's political/artistic aims."* Gidal's beliefs are scarcely unjustified. The slowness of certain segments of the film community in America to recognize European talents other than Peter Kubelka is both curious and disturbing. But while decrying the tactics of this North American alliance, Gidal shows he isn't above making similar power plays on behalf of those he sees as the true bearers of the avant-grail. Under the banner of

---

*"British Avant-garde Film," *Millennium Film Journal* #13 (Fall/Winter 1983-84), p. 12.

"structuralist/materialist" film practice, Gidal has marshalled several worthy names (e.g. Snow, Kurt Kren) alongside several other less worthy ones (Malcolm LeGrice, Gidal himself). All are seen as knights in battle in the holy war against the dragon of narrative "illusionism" that threatens the precious bodily fluids of all film culture today. Armed with a clutch of half-baked pseudo-theories concerning these works' presumed powers in revealing that images are not paradigms of reality but carefully constructed networks of imaginary relations, Gidal has dutifully impressed backward three-year-olds of all ages.

Gidal is not alone in attempting to wedge his way past the avant status quo—the better to carve out one all his own. A lower-keyed response to the same thing can be found in Peter Wollen's "Two Avant-Gardes" notion.* This attempt at accounting for certain nonconformist strains in non-co-op filmmaking—post-May '68 Godard, Straub and Huillet, classic forerunners like Eisenstein and Vertov—is little more than a marginally useful way of lumping certain semirelated figures together. It also provides a handy context for placing Wollen and Laura Mulvey's films on the highest conceivable level (as P. Adams Sitney has pointed out).

What neither Gidal nor Wollen provides is a route around this cultural impasse. Both acknowledge the American avant-establishment implicitly as an ultimate authority, but while one seeks to attack it head-on, the other attempts to appease it from the sidelines. Avoiding its traps entirely, logically enough, looms as the prospect before us. The filmmakers in the section that follows are neither part of the commercial mainstream nor of its "art" subsidiary. Some have one or two links with the co-op avant-garde on a methodological level without sharing that movement's current structural preoccupations. None of these films or filmmakers can be seen as linked to some epic configuration. Much needs to be said of the aesthetic/historical space that stands around them—which would in turn touch on other filmmakers, and other kinds of cinema.

Most of these films have been screened in the "Art et Essai" cinemas of Europe—a genre of exhibition that has no genuine equivalent in the United States. Neither part of the "art" house mainstream nor a co-op-type venue, they provide a space for the "different" that is also a means of cultural containment—a ghetto. No question of these films' failure to "reach" an audience when one has already been chosen via the "Art et Essai" route. It is an urban audience, college educated, thoroughly middle class.

The films of Werner Schroeter, Philippe Garrel, Luc Moullet, and Raul Ruiz do not seek such an audience—or any audience for that matter; they *wonder* who their audiences may be. All films are marked by the circulation of desire between spectator and spectacle. Whether it be James Benning or James Bond, you get what you pay for. Schroeter, Garrel, Moullet, and Ruiz

---

Studio International, November/December 1975, p. 171.

give no such assurance. They do not address themselves to segregated classes of spectators as do Spielberg or Frampton. They search. The process of that search might be said in and of itself to mark theirs as avant-garde works. But that in turn would only lay the groundwork for yet another assault on the avant-bastion. Best pass over questions of classification in silence. There are far too many pressing problems on the horizon.

WERNER SCHROETER.
Born in Georgenthal, Thuringia, 1945.

1967—*Verona oder Zwei Katzen* (8mm, b&w, 10 min., silent)
1968—*Callas Walking Lucia* (8mm, b&w, 3 min., silent)
Callas—Text Mit Doppelbeleuchtung (8mm, b&w, 5 min., silent)
Maria Callas Portrait (8mm, b&w and color, 17 min., sound-on-tape)
Mona Lisa (8mm, b&w and color, 35 min., sound-on-tape)
Maria Callas Singt 1957 Rezitativ und Arie der Elvira aus Ernani 1844 von Giuseppe Verdi (8mm, b&w, 15 min., sound-on-tape)
Ubungen mit Darstellern (8mm, b&w, 27 min., silent)
La Morte d'Isotta (8mm, color, 15 min., sound-on-tape)
Himmel Hoch (8mm, b&w, 12 min., sound-on-tape)
Paula "Je Reviens" (8mm, color, 35 min., sound-on-tape)
Grotesk-Burlesk-Pittoresk (8mm, color and b&w, 60 min., silent) co-director Rosa Von Praunheim
Faces (8mm, b&w, 20 min., silent)
Aggressionen (16mm, b&w, 22 min.)
Neurasia (16mm, b&w, 41 min.)
Argila (16mm, color, b&w, two-screen projection, 36 min.)
Virginia's Death (16mm, b&w, 9 min., silent)
1969—*Eika Katappa* (16mm, color, 144 min.)
Nicaragua (16mm, b&w, 80 min.)
1970—*Der Bomberpilot* (16mm, color, 65 min.)
Anglia (16mm, color, unfinished)
Salome (16mm, color, 81 min.)

1971—*Macbeth* (Video, color, 60 min.)
Funkausstellung 1971—Hitparade (Video,
unreleased)
Der Tod der Maria Malibran (16mm, color, 104 min.)
1973—*Willow Springs* (16mm, color, 78 min.)
1974—*El Angel Negro* (16mm, color, 71 min.)
1975—*Johannas Traum* (16mm, color, 30 min.)
1976—*Flocons d'Or* (16mm, color, 163 min.)
1978—*Regno di Napoli* (35mm, color, 130 min.)
1980—*Palermo oder Wolfsburg* (35mm, color, 175 min.)
Weisse Reise (16mm, color, 52 min.)
Generalprobe (16mm, color, 90 min.)
1981—*Der Tag der Idioten* (35mm, color, 97 min.)
Concilio d'Amore (35mm, color, 96 min.)
1984—*Der Lachende Stern* (16mm, color, 110 min.)

None of Werner Schroeter's films are currently
available in the United States. Distribution inquiries should
be made through Filmverlag der Autoren and Munic Film.

Next to the box office conquests of Lucas and Spielberg, the rise of the
"New German Cinema" was unquestionably the key film event of the late
1970s. Part figure of journalistic fancy, part plain undeniable fact, this ready-
made artistic/commercial context quickly found the names of Rainer Werner
Fassbinder, Wim Wenders, Werner Herzog, and Hans-Jurgen Syberberg
splayed across the international filmmaking horizon with an impact far
beyond that afforded the French "new wave" of a decade earlier. Still, in
the midst of this cultural frenzy, one name remained (and remains) curiously,
conspicuously overlooked—Werner Schroeter.

"Few of us have had the opportunity to make films that didn't borrow
from Schroeter," Fassbinder declared in an article published in the West
German press (*Frankfurter Rundschau*, Feb. 24, 1979) on the occasion of
the release of Schroeter's **Regno di Napoli**. From their very first appearance,
such Schroeter films as **Eika Katappa** and **Salome** made an unprecedented
impression on the entire German postwar cultural scene. Rejecting anything
smacking of conventional realism, obsessively devoted to ritual and gesture,
these makeshift "camp" extravaganzas—wild pastiches of grand opera and
classical theater—brought a long-dormant expressionist tradition back to
full bloom with a new comic/ironic twist. Shunning ordinary standards of
technical polish (in a way obviously indebted to the work of Jack Smith)
these low-rent fantasies freey mixed "high" and "low" dramatic forms (Kleist,
Shakespeare, and Oscar Wilde recast as soap opera) and musical expression
(classical masterpieces cheek-by-jowl with Motown and Caterina Valente)
in a manner designed both to incite and to impress.

The Pop Art *Strurm und Drang* of Fassbinder's **The Bitter Tears of Petra
Von Kant** (1972) finds its origins here, as do the benumbed theatrics

of Herzog's **Heart of Glass** (1976). Schroeter's peerless taste in rock 'n' roll is echoed in Wenders's somewhat more conventional disc jockeyings. Likewise his decor ideas are reflected in the slightly less *outré* trappings of Daniel Schmid. As for Hans-Jurgen Syberberg, dismissed outright by Fassbinder as nothing more than "an extremely capable Schroeter imitator,"* there is no question that the epic designs of his **Ludwig** (1972) and **Parsifal** (1982) would not have been possible had Schroeter not gotten there first. Syberberg himself unashamedly acknowledges this fact in **Ludwig** in a scene where the spirit of Richard Wagner (played by a woman) rises out of the mists of time to declare that his operas will not truly come to life until Schroeter stages them (which the filmmaker/director did not get around to doing until 1979 with a stage production of "Lohrengrin").

That an artist so central has been shunted to one side so blithely may seem incredible, except for one important fact. The majority of Schroeter's works have been in 8 and 16mm. This, in Fassbinder's view, has made it possible for "the culture machine" to label Schroeter an "underground" filmmaker—less a generic description than a form of *sotto voce* dismissal. Industry "professionals" need not take such an "amateur" seriously. This would logically leave the door open for Schroeter to align himself with the co-op avant-garde. But, while inspired by that movement, he has never, beyond his early years, truly been a part of it. This, in turn, is neither to say that Schroeter is an "art" director *manqué*. As his recent sorties into 35mm, such as **Palermo oder Wolfsburg** and **Der Tag der Idioten**, have shown, nothing is clear-cut about Schroeter but his talent and his commitment to utilizing it precisely as he sees fit.

A psychology student at the University of Mannheim, Schroeter first became attracted to the idea of filmmaking when he saw Gregory Markopoulos's **Twice a Man** at Knokke-Le Zoute in 1963. But the film courses offered by the universities, Schroeter soon discovered, were of no use to him whatsoever. Taking matters into his own hands, he began making his first works, starting at a level that might be described as somewhere *below* scratch. He filmed still photographs of Maria Callas with his 8mm camera and used her recordings as accompaniment during projection of the resultant works. Callas, whom Schroeter has called "the erotic vision of my childhood … total passion," became the nexus of all his cinematic concerns (much like Maria Montez for Jack Smith) as he began to explore new cinematic terrain.

At first it was little more than a matter of filming faces and gestures for Schroeter—capturing (and creating) moods and moments with the help of his friends. Then little dramatic scenes began to take shape about these bits and pieces, recalling certain moments in opera and theater performances that had impressed Schroeter. Gradually, arrangements of such moments,

---

*Gerard Courant, *Werner Schroeter* (Goethe Institute/Cinemathéque Française, 1982), p. 107.

without the narrative and character filler that usually surrounded them, became the very substance of the work. Music played a central role in all of this, not merely supplementing action and image, but shaping it as well. **Eika Katappa**, for example, offers a melange of Verdi, Penderecki, Beethoven, Bellini, Strauss, Puccini, and Bizet, with the tango music used on the soundtrack of Buñuel's **Un Chien Andalou** and the Drifters' "Save the Last Dance for Me" thrown in for good measure, all against the backdrop of highly stylized posings and acting-outs. By its very force each new musical cue propels the film forward while keeping it from achieving definitive shape, stopping and starting, again and again.

It is the performers, however, and their gradually developing style that stand at the heart of Schroeter's project at this point in his career. All of the most important of them are women. All are adept at bizarre poses, grand gestures, lavishly overwrought displays of suffering and passion—the entire panoply of "camp" acting at its most baroque. Capable of both intense concentrated effort and free moments of sheer improvisation, they grip the screen with an uncanny authority. In **Der Tod der Maria Malibran** the fruits of such labors are displayed to their best advantage. Magdalena Montezuma (a striking, large-boned *grand dame*, Schroeter's chief interpreter) takes on the role of the legendary nineteenth-century opera star, with Schroeter regulars Christine Kaufmann and Ingrid Caven, aided by Candy Darling (who at one point warbles "St. Louis Blues") as special guest star in attentive support. As everything from Ambrose Thomas operas to Marlene Dietrich theater songs let loose on the soundtrack, parallels are drawn through rigorously choreographed bits of dramatic by-play (as with Jack Smith, there is no acting in the conventional sense of the term) between the diva's passing and the thousand deaths she had suffered before on the stage.

This is all, of course, great fun for opera aficionados, but there is an underlying seriousness to all this seeming nonsense. The images of suffering and passion that Schroeter plays with here all proceed from an ideological sphere that identifies them as feminine and upper class. By depriving them of psychological resonance—the means by which such notions are propelled past representational specificity to reach the category of what is generally referred to as "the universal"—Schroeter forges them into pure icons of dramatic affectivity. Laid bare in this fashion, these socially acceptable images of suffering are displayed (*and* enjoyed) for what they really are— mindless fetish objects. Genuine suffering and passion (women in specific culturally identified circumstances) will have to be considered in relation to these images on another plane. The status of representations as ultimate expressions of emotion is thus neatly undermined. It is for this reason that it is not surprising to hear Schroeter speak of his interest in cultural reference through musical forms as a "weapon against the consumer society" or of his own homosexuality as "a reaction to a materialist milieu." Hardly unexpected either in this light to discover Schroeter moving away from such stylish charades to larger forms of social engagement in his more recent works, particularly **Regno di Napoli** and **Palermo oder Wolfsburg**.

Tracing the lives of a group of Neopolitan slum dwellers from 1944 to 1977, **Regno di Napoli** (*Kingdom of Naples*) appears as something of a shock to those who had mistaken Schroeter for little more than a specialist in stylistic affectation. Detailing a world that bears nary a hint of glamour, it would also suggest a formal abandonment of expressionist romanticism in favor of a full-blown revival of the neo-realist aesthetic. But in the film's opening moments, in which a hand-held camera wanders through deserted urban ruins, it is clear that Schroeter has not abandoned the world of Casper David Friedrich; he has simply, daringly, transformed it—turned German inwardness outward.

The world that unfolds before us for the next two hours is desperate and squalid. Men search for jobs; women are forced into prostitution. Some suffer and die in sordid circumstances; others manage to squeeze their way into the lower echelons of the *petit bourgeoisie*. Both the Catholic church (the emotional refuge of women) and the Communist party (the emotional refuge of men) are seen as inadequate social outlets for a faith in life their followers, far more than their organizers, believe in. Over it all hangs Schroeter's passionately perceptive eye—all the more effective for remaining bone-dry at all times.

We are far from the cinema of a DeSica, whose compassion for his characters is not without an occasional touch of condescension—an inevitable by-product of his thoroughly middle-class point of view. The mysticism that infests a Rossellini is likewise absent here. Schroeter does not crave after something ineffable hovering just outside the frame—he is far too concerned with what's right there on the inside. A viewpoint more akin to Visconti can be seen in Schroeter, however, particularly in relation to André Bazin's remark that the protagonists of **La Terra Trema** were less Sicilian fishermen than "renaissance princes." Schroeter doesn't carry things quite that far. Yet there is a deliberate bearing with which his characters carry themselves that marks them as slightly other than that which their circumstances suggest. This does not (as in Visconti's case) spring from a gulf between the creator and his characters' real-life correlatives. Rather it links up with the imaginative register in which Schroeter places his people and their experiences. Passion and suffering in **Regno di Napoli** do not proceed from a fantasy context as in opera, but are, rather, grounded in the historical reality of postwar Italy. All that Schroeter wishes to do is win for that reality the sense of mythic grandeur automatically seen as the natural birthright of upper-class art forms (opera, novels, etc.).

In the last scene of the film, a prostitute who has appeared periodically throughout the action is beaten and robbed for what apparently is far from the first time. Rising from the ground she strides the nighttime streets crying in convulsive despair. It is the grand summation of all we have seen throughout the film. It is also entirely operatic in form, clearly referring to Visconti's **Senso**, whose finale also featured a woman wailing on a deserted street. But she was a nineteenth-century aristocrat who had lost the man she loved—an operatic figure *par excellence.* Here we see nothing more than a common prostitute—a banal event filmed in documentary style. Yet in Schroeter's hands grace and grandeur are never absent. We resist the full dramatic pull of the moment at our own risk.

In **Palermo oder Wolfsburg**, Schroeter's efforts achieve even sharper focus. The plot derives from an actual incident in which a Sicilian youth was convicted of committing a murder in Germany, where he had emigrated in the hope of finding work. At the trial, the enormous disparity between that which he came to and that which he left behind was emphasized by the defense counsel in the hopes of explaining the sense of alienation that inspired the tragedy.

It would be easy to imagine what a Fassbinder would make of such material—a terse, almost cartoon-like melodrama in which social observations would be scored off in brisk, businesslike fashion. Schroeter's approach is far from concise or specific. An epic film divided into three self-contained, hour-long parts, **Palermo oder Wolfsburg** begins with its ostensible subject only to reach far beyond it in the direction of an ultimate vision of the life experience.

In the first section we are introduced to our hero, Nicola Zarbo (played by a young non-professional of the same name), and shown about his hometown, the desperately poor Sicilian village of Palma di Montechiaro. As in **Regno di Napoli**, Schroeter allows us to observe character and context in the simplest way. We see Nicola moving through his world and learn of its extents (sentimental) and limits (economic). The limits eventually win out. Observing his father's decline into alcoholic despair, Nicola resolves that the same fate will not befall him. He emigrates to Germany and gets a job in a Volkswagen factory.

At the hostel where the workers rest at night, Nicola discovers many other immigrants in the same position he is in, trying to adjust to an alien environment. He discovers a refuge of sorts in a cafe run by an Italian woman (Ida di Benedetto) sympathetic to his plight. Still, Nicola finds himself prone to melancholy—until he captures the attention of a young German girl (Brigitte Tilg) he is attracted to. Half-worldly, half-naive, this kittenish teenager appears at first to have some degree of genuine interest in Nicola. But at a local dance they attend her pose is revealed to be a sham—she only pretended attraction to him in order to provoke two other suitors. When these two (both Germans) confront Nicola outside the dance hall and begin to taunt and insult him, he takes out his pocket knife and calmly, as if in some sort of trance, stabs them to death.

Nicola sits at the trial (the third section of the film), his hands clasped in prayer, saying nothing in his own defense. That role is taken up by his

Nicola Zarbo in
Palermo oder Wolfsburg,
by Werner Schroeter

lawyer (Magdalena Montezuma in an uncharacteristically subdued performance). Drawing upon a host of character witnesses, she quickly establishes
extenuating circumstances in Nicola's case. The cafe owner is especially
impressive, explaining the boy's unfamiliarity with German (he may not
have known what was being said to him at the murder scene) and citing
the past histories of the deceased—rowdy louts who had caused trouble at
her cafe on other occasions. Nicola would appear to have been saved, until
the very moment the "not guilty" verdict is announced. Rising from his seat,
trembling with fury and indignation he cries at the top of his lungs, "I killed
them! I killed them because I wanted to!" Hauled away by courtroom guards,
his fate is sealed.

   This, in condensed form, is the *plot* of **Palermo oder Wolfsburg**. The
film itself is something else entirely—a network of textual subtleties no linear
retelling can possibly account for. There is, for example, the disposition of
the camera in each section of the work—a presence so strong as to suggest
the status of a character, which in many ways it is. In Palma di Montechiaro

it is chiefly hand-held, pacing the streets and byways of the village with
Nicola as he encounters friends and neighbors in small scenes that never
quite take the form of dramatic vignettes. Drama comes more sharply into
play in the second section, in Germany, where the image is, for the most
part, still—firmly grounded to observe the world of the "economic miracle"
with bitter clarity. In the third section, tracking shots predominate as the
full play of Schroeter's expressionism takes over. Just as the lawyer's defense
attempts to account for Nicola in a manner the bourgeoisie will accept, so
the *mise en scène* traffics in (and parodies) bourgeois dramatic forms.

The cafe owner's testimony is staged like an aria. When Nicola falls
asleep during the proceedings his dreams pop up as matter-of-fact realities
on the screen. Spectators who had earlier in the trial shot him hostile looks
are seen suddenly leaping about and grimacing wildly. A sense of the fantastic
has suddenly taken over the entire film. Not that it hadn't peeked out from
time to time before, as for example in a perfectly naturalistic moment in the
trial when a cathedral Nicola had fashioned out of toothpicks in his prison
cell is brought into the courtroom with ceremonial gravity as proof of his
strength of character. Then there is the perfectly straightforward shot that
opens the film's second section, of Nicola arriving before the enormous
gates of the Volkswagen factory, an ordinary long-shot in bright sunshine.
Nonetheless, Schroeter makes it plain that what we see before us is nothing
less than the modern equivalent of the vampire's castle in Murnau's **Nos-
feratu**. An equally striking bit of textual unsettlement can be found even
earlier, in the Palma di Montechiaro section, when Nicola visits one of his
friends who is having a music lesson. The home of the music teacher is
ablaze with hundreds of lighted candles on the floor and the furniture. "No,
no," he tells a student, "You must understand. Opera is not Verdi. Opera
is Bellini—Vincenzo Bellini!"

Dealing with these and other such moments as sudden eruptions of
ambiguity in an otherwise straightforward narrative would be a simple matter
were it not for an additional force that permeates the core of **Palermo oder
Wolfsburg,** directly connected to the shifting camera disposition mentioned
earlier. Over and above all its other subjects—cultural clashes, economic
oppression, the demoralization of postwar German industrial society—the
love of the filmmaker for his star predominates. Schroeter is plainly transfixed
by the sight of Nicola Zarbo, the camera becoming a corporeal presence
as it follows him, attends to him, *caresses* him. There is a well-established
tradition for such cinematic practice as far as heterosexuality is concerned
(e.g. Godard and Anna Karina, Rossellini and Ingrid Bergman). For homosexuality, however, there is none. Schroeter's insistence on establishing one—
especially at a time when all such efforts are placed critically under the
suspect heading of voyeuristic fetishization—is doubly daring. But it is inextricably tied to the film's meaning and purpose at every level. To ignore this
love is the exact equivalent of German society's wish to ignore Nicola, which

is precisely what it accomplishes in the act of defending him. As Schroeter films it, it is society, not Nicola, that is on trial here. Society must turn him into that good-but-misunderstood common man in order to cover its own tracks. It must do all in its power to see Nicola's crime as anything but the anarchistic act of protest it actually is.

Schroeter does not ask our pity or sympathy. To do so would be, simply, to assume the lawyer's role. In demanding our love instead Schroeter puts the entire situation on another plane. We are not *here* in Palma di Montechiaro, or in Wolfsburg, or the courtyard, but rather in a perpetual *elsewhere*, that area between the spectator and the screen of which Godard speaks so frequently, where love of Nicola can flourish in defiance of society, of culture, of circumstance.

This form of cinema is perilous. **Regno di Napoli**, arriving as it did on the heels of any number of reinvestigations of Italy's past (**Novecento, Amarcord, We All Loved Each Other So Much**), was clearly a savage critique of such lulling nostalgic spectacles. Instead of bittersweet regret Schroeter's film offered only convulsive horror. These are not the problems of the middle class to which the "art" film is invariably addressed. **Palermo oder Wolfsburg** is a linear narrative with characters in a specified social context. This is not the mode the academic bourgeoisie—with which the co-op avant-garde is presently allied—takes seriously. And as for sexuality, it offers none of the consumer pleasures (even those of slumming) recognized by upscale urban homosexual pseudo-culture.

Schroeter, for his part, appears to have accepted his outsider status completely. His recent films have found him taking off in any number of directions, both new and old. **Weisse Reise** returns Schroeter to his primitive past. Actors before a painted backdrop go through the motions of a tale of two sailor lovers and their travels throughout the world, while Bulle Ogier's voice describes their adventures on the soundtrack. **Generalprobe** and **Der Lachende Stern** are both made up of documentary impressions—the first of a dance festival in France, the second of the Manila film festival and life in the Philippines in general. Of his 35mm works, **Concilio d'Amore**, a film based on Antonio Salines's production of a play by Oscar Panizza, has been regarded as a retreat over familiar Schroeter ground. **Der Tag der Idioten**, on the other hand, is more of a departure.

Carole Bouquet, in what she herself rightfully regards as the first performance of her career (she was no more than a mannequin in **Cet obscur objet du desir** and **For Your Eyes Only**), stars as a young woman disappointed in love who decides to have herself declared insane as an act of social protest. The question of whether she actually *is* insane, usually asked in an "art" film context (e.g. **Repulsion, Lilith**), is explored by Schroeter as he brings to bear all the stylistic notions of his early works (particularly **Flocons d'Or** and **Willow Springs**) on an ostensibly naturalistic context. But just as in **Palermo**, with its reversal of society/criminal relations, the status of sanity is put to the test in a *mise en scène* that refuses to separate what is "real" from what is "imaginary." As much as anything else, this fundamental refusal stands at the very heart of Schroeter's project; it is the reason he continues in spite of the indifference that has always served as the best defense against its power, honesty, and truth.

Carole Bouquet in
Der Tag der Idioten,
by Werner Schroeter

PHILIPPE GARREL.
Born in Paris, 1948.

1966—*Les Enfants desaccordes* (35mm, b&w, 15 min.)
           Droit de visite (35mm, b&w, 15 min.)
1967—*Anémone* (16mm, color, 60 min.)
           Marie pour memoire (35mm, b&w, 80 min.)
1968—*Le Revelateur* (35mm, b&w, 60 min., silent)
           La Concentration (35mm, color, 103 min.)
           Actua 1 (35mm, b&w, 10 min., lost)
1969—*Le Lit de la vierge* (35mm, b&w, scope, 103 min.)
1972—*La Cicatrice interieure* (35mm, color, 60 min.)
1973—*Athanor* (35mm, color, 20 min., silent)
1974—*Les Hautes solitudes* (35mm, b&w, 75 min., silent)
1975—*Un Ange passe* (35mm, b&w, 80 min.)
1976—*Le Berceau de cristal* (35mm, color, 80 min.)
1977—*Voyage au Jardin des Mortes* (35mm, color, scope,
           55 min.)
1978—*Le Bleu des origines* (35mm, b&w, 50 min., silent)
1982—*L'Enfant secret* (35mm, b&w, 95 min.)

1983—*Liberte, la nuit* (35mm, color, 90 min.)
1984—*Rue Fontaine*—episode in *Paris vu par ... vingt
ans aprés* (16mm, b&w, 17 min.)

For a brief time during the late 1960s, Universal Pictures
distributed *Marie pour memoire*. None of Garrel's work
is presently available in the United States. Distribution
inquiries should be made through L'Institut National
de la Communication Audiovisuelle.

The image on the screen is black and white, silent, slightly grainy. It
is a close-up of a woman's face, beautiful, smiling and relaxed. She is staring
straight ahead at the camera (at us), her head lolling a bit from side to side.
A simple shot, unaffected and unadorned. Like most of the others in the
film that surrounds it, it displays this woman (her moods, her movements)
with absolute clarity. There is no story of any discernible kind attached to
this. For the most part we simply have this woman's image placed upon the
screen—her gaze seeming to challenge that of the machine. Occasionally
the woman is seen on a bed, tossing and turning as if unable to sleep.
Sometimes she speaks to someone just out of camera range. Other moments
find her sitting quietly, calmly, rocking her body to and fro, lost in thought.
The film's utter devotion to her is broken only on a handful of occasions,
when shots of two other women and one or two of a man appear like bits
of visual punctuation.

At a time when film theory has reached the status of a cultural obsession,
images like these arrive as answered prayers. We can see how they are put
together—easily, artlessly. They are up on the screen; we are down in the
audience. No trick of film craft, no artificial suturing of spectator to spectacle
violates this basic division. We are presented with nothing to make us believe
these images are other than or more than what they appear to be—except
perhaps for one fact: the woman we are looking at is Jean Seberg.

We are not looking at the image of an anonymous woman, but that of
a famous movie star. Her past performances are immediately brought to
bear; knowledge of her personal life becomes enmeshed in the process as
well. The film **Les Hautes solitudes**, by Philippe Garrel, was made in 1974.
Impossible to look at it today without meditating on Seberg's passing some
five years after it was made, for Garrel's camera sees Seberg honestly, as if
discovering her for the first time, as if Jean Seberg weren't already Jean
Seberg. Keeping within the boundaries of technical primitiveness (no sound,
no color, no story), Garrel allows us to see someone we haven't really seen
before. There were fleeting moments in **Saint Joan**, the last shot of **Bonjour
tristesse,** *many* of the shots in **A Bout de souffle**, but they never offered so
uninterrupted, so compassionate a view. Such conventional films, theory
tells us, like all narratives, involve the viewer in a network of imaginary
interchanges that only serve to create a fetishized relationship to spectacle.
Yet here we encounter much the same sort of situation in a different guise.

We are given no narrative whatsoever, but the entire film offers itself as a fetish object. Seberg's presence, of course, plays a large role in this, but not completely. For there is every reason to believe **Les Hautes solitudes** would produce the same results, the same degree of specular fascination, if an unknown performer—man or woman—were involved.

Consider another example, another Garrel image—more complex, in color, with sound. The woman (beautiful, unsmiling), viewed in medium long shot, is this time less well known. (Nico, singer with the Velvet Underground, actress in Warhol's **The Chelsea Girls** and **Imitation of Christ**, the blonde who took Marcello to the aristocrats' revels in **La Dolce Vita**). She is standing on the left side of the frame on a rocky, slightly elevated plain. She hugs the white coat she is wearing to her body in response to the evident cold. The wind howls across the landscape as dark clouds gather. Her long light-brown hair blows about as she stares off toward the right. Behind her, taking up most of the space in the shot, is an enormous circle of ice—a small frozen lake in the near distance. It is part of a visual motif that runs throughout the film **La Cicatrice interieure** (*Inner Scar*). These frozen wastes are echoed in other circular images, such as one of the mouth of a volcano. Circles of fire appear as well in another scene where a horse and rider are surrounded by flames on a desert plain. Then there are the circles the camera makes in nearly every scene of this hour-long spectacular, shot on location in some of the most exotic, far-off reaches of the globe—Iceland, the Canary Islands, Morocco, Death Valley. They mark the landscape just as Michael Snow's mechanized camera marks the air in **La Region centrale**. But unlike in that film, an atmospheric sense proceeds from these nominally technical maneuvers.

"I don't know how to explain," Henri Langlois confessed of Garrel's film, "suddenly all humanity is there, the whole earth talking. The earth in its primitive role of mother. But it isn't even the earth talking, it is the Humus."* Langlois's remarks are not overstatements. Garrel's film does produce a sense of awe—even though the means put at its disposal to do so are almost as primitive as those of **Les Hautes solitudes**. There are no trick shots or lavish sets as in **The Thief of Baghdad** or **Hercules Conquers Atlantis**—the two fantasy superproductions **La Cicatrice interieure** brings most immediately to mind in terms of spectacle and the sense of wonder engendered in the viewer. Each shot of Garrel's film may have been difficult to obtain from a logistical standpoint, yet each is set out on the screen in the lightest, most easygoing manner possible—like a child emptying the contents of his pockets and presenting each item in turn.

It might be possible to declare from this evidence that Philippe Garrel has managed to discover some *degree zero* of representation in which the most pared-down images manage to yield the most complex results—results

---

*"The Seventh Heaven," *Sight and Sound* (Autumn 1972), p. 182.

that current theory can in no way adequately account for. But Garrel can't quite claim full responsibility for bringing these effects about. The concept of works having "lives of their own" is always in the forefront of such efforts, the filmmaker to a large degree the servant of the act of cinematic inscription itself. Moreover, the returns to zero found in **Les Hautes solitudes** and **La Cicatrice interieure** are not the same; each is part of a constant process of discovery and regeneration.

Nico and Pierre Clementi in *La Cicatrice interieure*, by Philippe Garrel

Philippe Garrel began his career in 1966 at 18 years of age with two shorts and one featurette made for television but never broadcast. The three films that followed—**Marie pour memoire**, **Le Revelateur**, and **La Concentration**—immediately established his reputation and created a general impression of his ways and means that persists today (despite the many by-ways Garrel's career has taken over the years). Unlike their immediate predecessors (all fragmentary narratives of sorts), these works have few connections with anything resembling plot or character, though they do feature professional performers (among them Laurent Terzieff, Jean-Pierre Léaud, and Bernadette Laffont).

In **Marie pour memoire**, several youthful couples are viewed in sundry locations in and around Paris (apartment flats, city streets, vacant lots) in situations that hover on the edge of drama but never quite evolve along such lines. **Le Revelateur** takes things a step further. A silent mood piece, it features a man, a woman, and a child interacting in interior and exterior settings with a touch of quasi-religious imagery (the trio suggests a kind of "hippie" holy family). Throughout they appear before the camera more like figures in a painting or *tableau vivant* than those of a drama.

The camera's role as something more than a mere mechanical device for Garrel is even more apparent in **La Concentration**. A man and a woman in a single setting enact a kind of "primal scream" ritual (very much on the order of the "Living Theater") of birth, sexual discovery, and death. Regarded by the performers as something between a mirror and a corporeal presence, the camera becomes a species of weapon at the end of the film as the actors hurl themselves at it in a mime of suicidal annihilation.

The appearance of this loose trilogy was nothing short of a sensation in a French film scene that had had little it could truly call avant-garde since the Twenties. Critics soon saw links between Garrel's work and the films of that era, with the poetic tradition of Rimbaud, Cocteau, and the French symbolists seen as an additional source of influence. Yet while Garrel was no doubt aware of such a cultural heritage and (being the son of actor Maurice Garrel) hardly unacquainted with the film world as a whole, a sense of his creating these films out of whole cloth persists. The films were purely (painfully) personal, and alive with a sense of spontaneity and intuition. Moreover, no one (not even Warhol) had ever treated the camera quite in this way. With Garrel it was not a means, but an end in itself—a living thing, a totem in some bizarre ceremony.

"You go somewhere with people, bring a camera with you, and get into a collective psychosis, just like that ... with the camera," Garrel declared in an interview (*Afterimage* #2, Autumn 1970) in which he also noted, "Making the film is the most interesting [part]. What comes after it's made isn't very interesting." It would be a simple matter to dismiss such statements as mere dandyish phrasemaking were it not for the evidence provided by the films themselves. By placing the act of shooting on a primary plane, Garrel establishes a new species of spectator/spectacle relations. What we see is not directed at us, but back at the performers; any meaning that might be derived from these private rites comes into play on another level. The effect is similar in one sense to that of Jean Rouch's ethnographic works, like **Les Maîtres fous** and **La Chasse au Lion à l'Arc**. What is experienced has an entirely different meaning to those of us *outside* than it does to those participants up on the screen. But Rouch's films are culturally retrievable as educational documents. Garrel's films have no such utilitarian dimension. Despite their "name" casts there is no place for them on the "art" circuit. Despite their experimental methods they are too grandly scaled for the co-op avant-garde.

At the time of their first appearance, however, **Marie pour memoire**, **Le Revelateur**, and **La Concentration** did manage to achieve some level of identity, as their rejections of standard forms of cinematic consumption fed directly into the social and political atmosphere that would erupt in May 1968. Seen today, these three works—none of which are, in their maker's words, "socially or psychologically analytical"—nonetheless resonate with just such a point of view. In **Marie pour memoire**, when a character's political affiliations are described as "moralist, waiting for something better," it's almost tantamount to a trailer for the era to come.

During the events of May, Garrel (often as not accompanied by his aesthetic/spiritual father Jean-Luc Godard) filmed a newsreel of street clashes for the *Actualites revolutionnaires* (called **Actua 1**, this film has since been lost). In the period that followed he resumed his style of work as before, this time spreading it on a larger canvas. His nascent pre-'68 anarchy had blossomed by this point. "If I were to sit under a flag," he said in an interview, "I would sit under an anarchist flag.... Yes, I like black ... it's a rather beautiful color."

Le Lit de la vierge sits beneath this banner in its wholesale assault on the imagery of organized religion, with intimations of a desire to return to a more savage level of myth and symbol. Such ideas were not new to Garrel (both **Marie** and **Le Revelateur** contain suggestions of them), but here they take on a blatant form with Pierre Clementi and Zouzou in roles clearly meant to suggest Christ and the Virgin. Shot in Cinemascope and black and white on the rocky plains and desert wastes of North Africa, **Le Lit de la vierge** is nowhere near as straightforward in its imagery as (for example) Buñuel's **La Voie lactée** (produced the same year). Nevertheless, a scene in which the camera tracks through caves where anguished faces peer out, suggesting the suffering humanity Christ came to aid, is as close as Garrel has ever come to straightforward allegory. He balances gestures made in that direction with several scenes featuring less obvious by-play, such as one in which Zouzou regulates the rate at which Clementi eats a meal by barking out commands alternately to begin and to wait, and another where the two simply stand stark still on the desert at night while a song by Nico plays on the soundtrack.

La Cicatrice interieure pulled completely away from such referential specifics while providing even more provocative imagery (e.g. the shots of Nico detailed earlier). With Clementi, Nico, and Garrel himself as the leading players, roles were less performed than inhabited—filling screen space in the manner of living objects. Turning even further in this direction Garrel made **Athanor**, a series of *tableaux vivants* that began as a film 45 minutes long but that was eventually cut to 20 minutes. Garrel had reached some sort of dead-end.

Between 1974 and 1978, he worked to establish a new style. Shooting for Garrel was now more than ever "a privileged moment ... where we eliminate everything anecdotal and search for the essentials."* His subjects were simply his performers, most of whom were well-known film figures (Bulle Ogier, Anita Pallenberg, Maria Schneider, Dominique Sanda) noted

---

*Interview with Philippe Garrel, *Cahiers du cinéma* #204 (September 1968), p. 40.

for their receptiveness to off-beat filmmaking methods. Suggestions of character and incident were contrived on occasion, but by and large atmosphere was all. Images were spare, and sound an expendable element (two of the works made in this period are completely silent). There are, of course, precedents to this sort of cinematic portraiture—Warhol's **13 Most Beautiful Women** and **13 Most Beautiful Boys** (both circa 1964), and Gregory Markopoulos's **Galaxie** (1966). But none of these works exhibits the combination of artifice and artlessness that appeared to be Garrel's chief goal. The visual beauty that had seemed to come so easily to him before was now being held at arm's length. None of the shots in **Les Hautes solitudes** could be called "pretty." Yet there remains an obvious sense of attentiveness to his performers' every nuance. Everything converges on faces, bodies, and gestures, which in and of themselves speak.

Philippe Garrel's trajectory, toward increasingly spectacular visual forms climaxed by **La Cicatrice interieure** and returning to a simplicity even more fundamental than that with which he began, suggests a career that has gone beyond a full circle. It is for this reason that his latest efforts, **L'Enfant secret** and **Liberte, la nuit**, are not quite the complete departure they may appear at first. For the first time since his very earliest efforts Garrel has turned toward semi-naturalistic characters and situations. For the *very* first time he has crafted films intended for distribution and exhibition channels beyond those venues he has utilized in the past. But rather than a complete break with previous work, these new Garrel films suggest the desire to achieve synthesis—a summary of ways and means.

L'Enfant secret traces select moments in the relationship of a young couple (Anne Wiazemsky and Henri de Maublanc), complicated by her child from a previous liaison. But this perfectly ordinary (almost neo-realist) dramatic subject is given far from ordinary treatment. *Temps morts* predominate in a film divided into titled chapters: *La Césarienne-section, Le Derniere des guerriers, Les Forêts desenchantées, Le Cercle ophidian.* Any one of them would serve for an earlier Garrel film. Likewise the minimal plot's grazing against such elements as depression, breakdown, shock therapy, and drugs, appears as full-blown manifestations of the oppressive gloom and sense of dread common to the films from the 1974-1978 period.

Liberte, la nuit harbors a similar melodramatic sense, its action centering on clandestine leftist groups in France during the Algerian war, and a romantic triangle between an older man (Maurice Garrel), his estranged wife (Emmanuelle Riva), and a young woman with whom he becomes involved (Christine Boisson). Yet just as with **L'Enfant secret, Liberte la nuit** scuttles the high-level dramatic potential of such subject matter at every opportunity, such as in a scene in which a meeting between two people turns less on *their* interaction than on the movements of a white sheet hanging from a clothesline between them, dividing and redividing the screen space as the wind blows it this way and that.

Maurice Garrel and Christine
Boisson in *Liberte, la nuit,*
by Philippe Garrel

It would be possible to claim from all of the foregoing that Garrel has simply discovered a new means of marketing the techniques he developed earlier—transformed them into simple elements of style, salable to the "art" market. This would be a tenable conclusion were the European cinema not in the desperate situation it is today, suspended between international middlebrow, all-star efforts like **La Nuit de Varennes** and all-out attempts to beat the American commercial cinema at its own game with the likes of **La Balance** and **Diva**. An "art" film is anything but welcome in such an atmosphere.

The key to Garrel's evolution must be viewed over the long haul. At the time he began, the cultural context was still receptive to new talents. Thanks to the indulgence of a wealthy benefactor, Garrel and other filmmakers of like-minded disposition were able, for a time at Zanzibar films (the name of the production company with which he was associated in the Sixties and early Seventies), to spin out their most wildly utopian designs. May '68 and the atmosphere of spiritual disaffection that came in its wake changed all that. Though Garrel was hailed as heir apparent to Godard, the French cinema proved to have no place for him. All of Jean Eustache's **La Mamman et la putain** (1973) testifies to both the atmosphere of the period (Garrel calls the film "the masterpiece of my generation") and the aesthetic stagnation that now loomed as France's filmmaking legacy. Garrel's move in the direction of minimalism is one answer to that stalemate. His re-emergence today (like Godard's celebrated "return" to the cinema with **Passion** and **Prénom: Carmen**) is another. Garrel is in a sense wildly behind the times— finally "caught up" as it were with an "art" cinema that is no longer viable. But as with Schroeter, the circuitous route Garrel's career has taken reflects choices quite personal in nature. In his view, his latest works merely take the form of a "return to my autobiography which I had abandoned,"* a

---

*Interview with Philippe Garrel, *Cahiers du Cinema* #344 (February 1983), p. 23.

reference to Garrel's first three works, prior to the trio that sprung him to fame. As the rest of cinema—bloated beyond recognition, hideously disfigured by the hybridization brought on by video—appears to be on the verge of ending, the cinema of Philippe Garrel is at last *beginning*.

LUC MOULLET.
Born in Paris, 1937.

1960—*Un Steack trop cuit* (35mm, b&w, 19 min.)
1961—*Terres noires* (35mm, color, 19 min.)
1962—*Capito?* (35mm, color, 19 min.)
1966—*Brigitte et Brigitte* (35mm, b&w, 75 min.)
1967—*Les Contrebandieres* (35mm, b&w, 80 min.)
1971—*Une Adventure de Billy le Kid/A Girl Is a Gun*
         (35mm, color, 78 min.)
1975—*Anatomie d'un rapport/ Farther Than Sex* (16mm,
         b&w, 82 min.) co-director, Antonietta Pizzorno
1978—*Genèse d'un repas* (16mm, b&w, 117 min.)
1981—*Ma Premiere brasse* (16mm, b&w, 43 min.)
1982—*Introduction* (16mm, color, 8 min.)
1983—*Les Minutes d'un faiseur de films* (16mm, b&w,
         13 min.)
         Les Harves (16mm, color, 12 min.)
         Barres (16mm, color, 14 min.)

> In the late Sixties and early Seventies, *Les Contrebandieres* was distributed by New Yorker Films. It has since been deleted from their catalog. No other Moullet films are currently available in the United States. He distributes his films through his own company in Europe and elsewhere.

Among the *Cahiers du Cinéma* critics-turned-filmmakers, Luc Moullet is by all accounts the odd duck out. Never a part of the commercial mainstream (Truffaut, Chabrol, Rohmer), *success d'esteme/de scandale* status (Godard and Rivette's stock-in-trade) has somehow eluded him. Part of the reason for this is the relatively slow momentum of his career. Though Moullet began filmmaking at roughly the same time as his *Cahiers* confreres, he didn't produce his first feature until 1966, by which time the fabled French "new wave" had ebbed to a half-hearted ripple. Whether the filmmaking establishment (*any* filmmaking establishment) would be hospitable to Moullet's ideas at any time, however, is an open question. With a marginality that appears as much willed as imposed, Moullet has gone his own peculiar way with his quirky little clutch of works whose minuscule budgets, personal methodology, and limited exhibition access smack more than anything else of the co-op avant-garde. In all likelihood, however, Moullet would resist such a label. He has, after all, only been trying to make films in the best "new wave" tradition—quickly, cheaply, and technical polish be damned. Moreover, he has never sequestered himself from ordinary commercial channels. In fact, as his own distributor he has more often than not tried to enter the marketplace right along with the big boys—selling his films to whatever international distribution concern might take them, and providing them an English-language version (in the case of **Une Adventure de Billy le Kid**) or contriving flashy alternate titles (*A Girl Is a Gun, Farther Than Sex*) to attract potential interest. The only problem is that there have been few takers for films so temperamentally off-beat and visually threadbare. The situation is less a reflection on Moullet (who knows exactly what he's doing and why) than it is on the film establishment. In the profoundest way possible they simply don't know how to take a joke.

Objectively speaking, Moullet's **Les Contrebandieres** is little more than two women and a man scampering over a lot of rocks and grass in childlike games of pursuit and capture—part Mack Sennett, part Daffy Duck. In the silent era such primitive by-play would be perfectly acceptable. But with the coming of sound and with it the infusion of conventions derived from theatrical farce, film comedy has taken on an increasingly slick appearance. Even performers firmly rooted in the silent style (Jacques Tati, Jerry Lewis) have felt it necessary to gussie things up a bit with snazzy art direction and such. About all Moullet can afford are a few props and one or two makeshift costumes. But rather than try to pass off his unvarying medium long-shots as the visual feast they aren't, Moullet sends them up, as in one scene in **Les Contrebandieres** where one of the heroines, on the lam from a posse of Customs officials, pours a teaspoonful of alcohol over a pathetic clump of weeds and sets it alight. "The Customs were met with a wall of fire," she declares in voice-over narration as Moullet cuts to a shot of a genuine field fire obviously culled from another source.

This voice-over narration, a device Moullet relies on infinitely more than spoken dialogue in almost all his films, brings up the one area where he might be able to compensate for his visual deficiencies—aural wisecracks. But Moullet's verbal dexterity also falls short of mass-market acceptability. He has no Woody Allen-style checklist of trendy concerns to proffer, no Capra corn, no Lubitsch touch. Beneath its veneer of sub-adolescent japery, **Les Contrebandieres** is a deadly serious film about the arbitrary nature of borders and countries, and the absolute absurdity of the barter system. "Look closely," says the film's hero, a border guard who first pursues and then joins forces with a pair of women smugglers, "this used to be a totalitarian state." The camera is focused on a thoroughly nondescript mountain streamlet. It pans away very briefly to a patch of ground. "Now it was to know freedom and democracy," he declares in ringing tones, "All at once, everything would change." The camera returns to its first position. "Look at it now!"

For Moullet the anarchist, politics that are at the very heart of his enterprise are inextricably linked to his economic status. "I'm not necessarily in favor of low budget cinema," he once confessed in an interview (*Cahiers du Cinéma* #216, Oct. 1969). "What interests me is keeping to the same idea of cinema, making the most expensive or the cheapest film possible. Because in both cases it's possible to create an original economic orientation on the same level as the aesthetic or social one." What Moullet means by this in actual practice is outlined in an article he wrote for the February 1967 issue of *Cahiers*, "Film Is Only a Reflection of the Class Struggle." Written well in advance of the journal's sudden turn to the left *and* Godard's well-publicized conversion to Maoism, this position paper on cinematic alienation sees the phenomenon purely in terms of an oppression produced by imagery. "They make the exploited person believe that beautiful *external* elements can be integrated into his sad actual life. Insofar as the discovery of beauty creates happiness, it is important to discover true rather than false beauty within normal life." What this means for Moullet in terms of his actual film practice is utter guilelessness of *mise en scène* coupled with an appreciation of the everyday both in its banality and its absurdity. The latter—exemplified by the numerous, and from an ordinary filmmaking standpoint "unnecessary," scenes of eating and washing-up afterwards in **Les Contrebandieres**—is a category of activity that Moullet sees as a genuine force of engagement. As one of the heroines of **Brigitte et Brigitte** explains, there is no alienation in the absurd because the individual "must contribute in order to adopt it." In other words, an indulgent chuckle at a bit of Moullet nonsense like the field fire can in a way serve as a first small step toward representational sanity. Moullet, unlike the commercial system that surrounds him, has nothing to prove. He does not show off (see Spielberg, Coppola, Lucas, etc., on the one hand; Brakhage, Frampton, Sharits, etc., on the other), he *shows*. We may not be impressed, but we can't say we've been deceived.

The roots of Moullet's ideas are many. Though born in Paris he was for the most part raised in the countryside. This background doubtless accounts for his near-obsession with exterior settings and such taken-for-granted activities as cooking, eating, and sleeping arrangements. It also sets him well apart from the *Cahiers* crowd's efforts. With the exception of Godard (who in recent years has put Paris behind him in favor of the Swiss landscape) theirs is a city cinema par excellence. Moullet's countryside is something of a cinematic Third World. Were a Jane Fonda or Jack Nicholson to find themselves in it, the entire project would revolve around efforts to explain the landscape away in terms of their deluxe presences—a fitting backdrop for a thoughtfully raised eyebrow. In the avant-garde sphere, cosmic comminglings are generally the order of the day with Man, God, and Nature writ large over the landscape. Moullet's rocks are just rocks. His people are actors playing fictional characters. The process of this fiction, however, underscores the fact that said rocks are owned and/or bartered and/or caught up in a system of exchange through which these actor/

characters pass. In short, a paradigm of actual relations in the actual world—absurd as it at first may seem.

The disreputability of Moullet's vision in relation to the cinematic status quo is a by-product of his critical past. As a *Cahiers* contributor, Moullet was always the most vocal champion of the *outre*. An early enthusiast of Samuel Fuller (who makes a brief appearance as himself in **Brigitte et Brigitte**), Moullet embraced with equal ardor the extremes of Gerd Oswald (every one of whose B films "deserves a long review" in his estimation) and Douglas Sirk (far from the respected figure he is today when Moullet took him up in the late Fifties). As with all such ultra-*cineaste* tastes, Moullet's involves a mixture of cultural bravado and genuine sincerity. Nevertheless one aspect of these perceptions plainly spills over into his own work: Moullet recognized, as few of his *Cahiers* contemporaries did, that films are utilitarian commodities—designed for specific use by one audience or another according to needs that are purely class-based. The critic who rejects a Fuller or Sirk out of hand as beneath serious consideration is only exposing class prejudices, because technically their films are above reproach, and aesthetically as seriously intended as any films ever made for commercial concerns. What they don't feature are concessions to the *petit bourgeois* standards of taste and decorum (seeing violence and sentimentality as innately debased when offered in undisguised form). Moullet, in refusing to contrive an artificial sense of economic expenditure—the aesthetic potlatch around which most of cinema revolves—puts himself in the same vulnerable position. To the cinematic superstructure that surrounds him, his films are manifestly *insignificant.*

Moullet's efforts to create "an original economic orientation on the same level as the aesthetic and social one"* take other forms as well. **Une Adventure de Billy le Kid** was advertised and sold by Moullet as "the first French western," immediately bringing into play a wild confluence of elements. At the time of the production of Moullet's film, 1971, American westerns had for all intents and purposes bit the dust. The late Sixties had seen the genre eaten alive by television. As the Seventies marched on, its conventions became absorbed by other genres—principally the science fiction film (e.g. **Star Wars**). But while there was no longer an American public for such a film (Moullet's efforts to attract their attention with the alternate title **A Girl Is a Gun** and an English-language version constituting something on the order of an *acte gratuit*), there *was* a French public of *cineastes* to draw on. The only problem was that these viewers, unable to get enough of Ford, Hawks, Boetticher, etc., would likely as not reject Moullet's film out of hand as inauthentic. Moullet was no doubt taking into consideration the situation that had arisen in relation to Italian "spaghetti" westerns, initially rejected by western purists, then later accepted as a genre all their own.

---

*See the 1967 *Cahiers* article.

The Italian films, however, did have the saving grace of American stars like Clint Eastwood and Lee Van Cleef. Moullet had Jean-Pierre Léaud. In one sense this was a logical choice as Léaud possesses much of the gestural vigor associated with such American stars as Richard Widmark and Lee Marvin. Nevertheless, his is a naturalist tradition, incapable of embodying the sense of mythic grandeur common to the form. Moullet's sense of land-scape matched his star in falling short of the presumably intended goal as well—for reasons spelled out earlier. But in Moullet terms, that's the point. A western is nothing more than a bunch of people jumping over a lot of rocks. A French western would have to star someone like Jean-Pierre Léaud. In short, what he was offering was a virtual contradiction in terms—in all its dialectical materialist glory.

Moullet's innate contradictoriness crops up as well in relation to one sub-genre for which his limited means would appear ideally suited—the intimate film centering on the relationship of a couple. But Moullet's **Anatomie d'un rapport** proved to be devoid of the slick post-psychoanalytic introspection of a **Scenes from a Marriage** or the fashion-conscious urbanity

Jean-Pierre Léaud in *Une Adventure de Billy le Kid* (aka *A Girl Is a Gun*), by Luc Moullet

of an **Annie Hall**. Honest to a fault, Moullet produces naught but a reflection of his own squalor. The film (hilariously redubbed **Farther than Sex** for an American market that never materialized) centers on Moullet's affair with Antonietta Pizzorno, who appropriately serves as the film's co-director. Moullet plays himself on screen, but Pizzorno's role (in what might be described as the film's one concession to commercial values) is taken by Christine Hebert (the young starlet who under the name Rachel Kesterber played the female lead in **Une Adventure de Billy le Kid**). The displacement leads to unique consequences as Pizzorno can observe her situation objectively (she jumps into the film herself at the climax, commenting on the entire process), while Moullet is left helplessly in the midst of his own awareness. Tasteful anguish (Bergman) and bittersweet regret (Woody Allen) play no role whatsoever in a film of cheap apartments, unmade beds, and the painfully intimate spectacle of sexual dysfunction and the nearly insurmountable problems created in learning to give, accept, or comprehend the notion of physical pleasure.

　　Genèse d'un repas, by contrast, finds Moullet, for perhaps the first time in his career, with an ideal form for his sensibility. The subject is, as its title indicates, food (Moullet's reigning aesthetic fetish), specifically a meal consisting of an omelet, tuna fish, and a banana. The filmmaker's simple objective is to trace the routes these foodstuffs took to reach the table. But, Moullet

Genèse d'un repas,
by Luc Moullet

being Moullet, it is a highly idiosyncratic tour. Just as smuggling in **Les Contrebandieres** began as an amateur effort, then became an active occupation, then expanded to rub shoulders against every form of business on a worldwide level, so here idle curiosity leads to high adventure in what might be called a science fiction film about the Third World. **Genèse d'un**

repas is, of course, a documentary, and as such falls into systems of cinematic relations in which Moullet's financial limitations prove an asset rather than a liability. An opulently budgeted film about the lives of the poor would be something of an obscenity. This is not to say that Moullet spares us any painful truths. Our pain is simply at the mercy of the Lewis Carroll-like logic of late twentieth-century capitalism in which alienated labor is a way of life—in this case people involved in the production of basic foodstuffs that they can in no way consume with the matter-of-factness of the wealthy westerners whom they serve.

But while Moullet here turns his camera away from the manic frivolity of his comic features, **Genèse d'un repas** is not the ethnographic document that a Jean Rouch would bring back from such an excursion. It is significant that the two films Moullet refers to in relation to his own are Welles's **F for Fake** and Godard and Gorin's **Letter to Jane**—in all of cinema the two nominal documentaries most suspicious of the "truth" they seek to provide.

Despite this new-found cinematic lucidity **Genèse d'un repas** has met with much the same reception as other Moullet efforts—equal measures of respectful curiosity and blank incomprehension. Recent years have found him in a sort of full circle position—making short films as he did in his earliest days. One of them, however, **Ma premiere brasse**, suggests that even in today's increasingly desperate cinematic circumstances, Moullet will find a way. It is a film of Moullet teaching himself how to swim. He is in effect reduced to the bare minimum—his own body. But then, that's all that Chaplin and Keaton had when you come right down to it. It's a good place to be.

RAUL RUIZ.
Born in Puerto Mont, Chile, 1941.

1960—*La Maleta* (16mm, b&w, 40 min.)
1967—*El Tango de Viudo* (16mm, b&w, 70 min.)
1968—*Tres Tristes Tigres* (35mm, b&w, 105 min.)
1969—*Militarismo y Tortura* (16mm, b&w, 40 min.)
　　　　La Catenaria (unfinished)
1970—*¿Que Hacer?* (16mm, color, 90 min.) Co-directors
　　　　Saul Landau, James Becket, Nina Serrano, and
　　　　Billy Yahraus.
1971—*La Colonia Penal* (16mm, b&w, 75 min.)
　　　　Ahora Te Vamos a Llama Hermano (16mm, b&w,
　　　　20 min.)
　　　　Nadie Dijo Nada (16mm, color, 135 min.)
1972—*La Expropriación* (16mm, color, 60 min.)
　　　　Los Minuteros (16mm, b&w, 15 min.)

1972—*Boesia Popula, La Teoría y La Práctica* (16mm,
b&w, 15 min.)
1973—*Nueva Canción Chilena* (16mm, b&w, 15 min.)
El Realismo Socialista (16mm, color, b&w,
225 min.)
Palomita Brava (16mm, b&w, 60 min.)
Palomita Bianca (35mm, color, 134 min.)
Abastecimiento (35mm, b&w, 15 min.)
1974—*Dialogue d'exiles* (16mm, color, 100 min.)
1975—*Le Corps dispersé et le monde à l'envers* (16mm,
color, 90 min.)
1976—*Sotelo* (16mm, color, 15 min.)
1977—*La Vocation suspendue* (16mm, color, b&w,
90 min.)
Colloque de chiens (35mm, color, 18 min.)
1978—*L'Hypothèse du tableau volé* (35mm, b&w, 67 min.)
Les Divisions de la nature (16mm, color, 28 min.)
1979—*Petit manuel de l'histoire de France* (video, b&w,
100 min.)
Des grands événements et des gens ordinaires
(16mm, color, 60 min.)
Images du débat (video, color, 88 min.)
Jeux (video, color, 60 min.)
1980—*Le Jeu de l'oie* (16mm, color, 30 min.)
La Ville nouvelle (16mm, color, 10 min.)
L'Or gris (16mm, color, 120 min.)
Teletests (video, color, 3 min.)
Pages d'un catalogue (video, color, 45 min.)
Fahlström (video, color, 30 min.)
1981—*Le Borgne* (16mm, color); 1 (20 min.); 2 (11 min.);
3 (25 min.); 4 (15 min.); 16 planned future episodes
The Territory (35mm, color, 110 min.)
Le Toit de la baleine (35mm, color, 90 min.)
Images de sable (video, color, 15 min.)
1982—*Les Trois couronnes du Matelot* (35mm, color,
117 min.)
Ombres chinoises (video, color)
Le Petit theatre (video, color)
Querelle des jardins (16mm, color, 26 min.)
Classification des plantes (16mm, color, 26 min.)
1983—*Lettre d'un cineaste ou Le Retour d'un amateur*
(16mm, color, 12 min.)
Berenice (35mm, b&w, 105 min.)
La Ville des pirates (35mm, color, 125 min.)

1984—*Point de Fuite* (35mm, b&w, 90 min.)
La Présence Réelle
in preparation:
Manoel et l'Ile des Merveilles
Voyage d'un main
L'Eternel mari
La Plage a falesa
Dans un miroir
Treasure Island
Madame Bovary

None of Ruiz's films are available in the United States at present.
Distribution inquiries should be made through L'Institut
National de la Communication Audiovisuelle and
Les Films du Passage.

Imagine a cinema unruled by manmade laws of consumption, so vast in scope that no single system of analysis could ever hope to account for it. It stretches out endlessly across countries and languages, fictional and documentary forms, 16mm, 35mm and video formats, works both large and small. The creator of this cinema is similarly multifaceted—a chameleon-like creature sometimes dominating his *mise en scène*, but more often taking a role on the sidelines. Correspondingly, this authorial voice varies in tone, not just from project to project, but within individual works themselves. Deadly serious one moment, it turns wildly satirical the next—no predicting the circumstances. Most disturbing of all, however, are the equally unpredictable moments when this voice falls silent. It is as if the film were merely a functional entity, an audiovisual unit needing no anchor for its ideas—a cinema of itself, a cinema of cinema.

The name of this cinema is Raul Ruiz. A Chilean émigré who for the past eight to nine years has made France his main base of operations, he is the nominal author of a group of works so stimulating and provocative that, while their public exposure has thus far been limited, awareness of their existence has proven sufficient cause for critical attention. This is perfectly appropriate, for dealing with Ruiz is coming to grips, not so much with an individual or a particular work, but with an *idea*—a cinematic myth.

Of the basic facts little is in dispute. A student of law and theology who began his artistic career in the theater, Ruiz entered filmmaking with relatively modest mainstream goals. Of his early feature **Tres Triste Tigres** (not to be confused with Guillermo Cabrera Infante's novel of the same name) Ruiz spoke of a desire to create "a film in which Chileans could recognize themselves" (*Afterimage* #10, Autumn 1981). But what form this identity would take, and toward what use it might be put, quickly became a complex question. A committed leftist, Ruiz became involved in the making of the collaborative film **¿Que Hacer?**, a mixture of documentary and fiction principally focusing on the Chilean elections that would see Marxist Salvatore

Allende made president. "We thought we were making a film to help a movement," Ruiz said of the project, "but we didn't really know what the movement was about." This doubt gradually became coupled with Ruiz's own uncertainties about his exact role as an intellectual: "Artistic activity is very difficult to explain and in relation to politics there has to be an experimental attitude."* It is this very attitude that Ruiz realized he had to take up. "After ¿Que Hacer? I wanted to devote myself to a personal 'irresponsible' film quite divorced from Chilean reality." The work he chose was an adaptation of Franz Kafka's *In the Penal Colony*. "If I had to defend myself in a court of law," Ruiz said, "I would say it was a metaphor on conditions in Latin America."

Ruiz's remark is a key to his entire outlook—now as then. Few would consider Kafka's novella "irresponsible," its vision of the legal system as an instrument of torture being in many obvious ways a metaphor for many Latin American situations (in the case of Chile it proved to be an ominous foretelling of the repression to come in the wake of Allende's overthrow by the fascists a few years later). But Ruiz's invocation of the notion of defense brings with it another configuration involving the problems faced by all Latin American intellectuals, more often than not operating under the heel of an oppressive right-wing political regime. This circumstance is directly linked to the fabulist tradition of which Ruiz is a part, which has produced such writers as García Márquez, Borges, and Bioy-Casares. This tradition, with its propensity for allegorical fantasy, provides a freer forum for political protest than would a naturalistic one. The "fantastic" in this context serves as a smokescreen for the very real sentiments behind it. The fabulist tradition is common to authoritarian right-wing regimes. With the Left in power in Chile (albeit temporarily) the direction of anti-authoritarian protest would be altered—leading to Ruiz's cryptic remark.

Yet another element is involved here, for in Ruiz's eyes, all social problems devolve from institutional power in all its forms. Speaking of his leftist roots, Ruiz noted his own difficulties in this regard: "I find it impossible not to cry during certain Stalinist films—like the scene in Dovzhenko where a man is expelled from his community and the party representative tells his son, 'Don't worry, now the party is your father.' This moves me and, however horrible it may be in political films, I am not afraid of it; I think the drive involved is very important and meaningful" (*Afterimage* #10, 1981). This might suggest that Ruiz would see his role along Fassbinderian lines—engaging himself with emotionally charged material all the better to deal with its emotional effect. But the exact opposite is the case. Ruiz's work is the last word in urbane sophisticated cool, its ironies so dry yet so delicately stated that their exact effect can't be gauged with any certainty—"irresponsibility" incarnate.

*Malcolm Coad, "Between Institution: Interview with Raul Ruiz," *Afterimage* #10 (Autumn 1981), p. 103.

This disposition to irreverence is at the heart of the troubles Ruiz faced with his first post-Chilean work, **Dialogue d'exiles**. A documentary on the plight of Chilean leftists like Ruiz himself who in the wake of the CIA-sponsored fascist coup that overtook their country were scattered to the far corners of the globe, it was expected to be a work of straightforward political protest. But Ruiz's film raised hackles in leftist circles for its less-than-rosy picture of a once united political front. As far as Ruiz was concerned, however, changes in circumstances had brought about changes in character and outlook in a logical way. "Once the revolutionary process is halted," he explained, "each [person] reintegrates into his class, the *petit bourgeois* into the *petite bourgeoisie*, the worker into the working class and the intellectual into the intellectual class."

Ruiz's own redirection of energies was now in order. He was literally a man without a country. There was still the *other* country to which all intellectuals of his class belonged—the arts. But rather than declare his exiled status as an aesthetic spectacle in and of itself, situating his ideas in a *mise en scène* of estrangement and regret (e.g. Polanski, Skolimowski, Miloš Forman), Ruiz chose instead to absent himself—to disappear into the field of television production. There he took on assignments of every type— historical recreations, documentaries, adaptations of literary works, original ideas of his own—the entire run of the European television mill. Yet anonymous as the context might be, the results were as personal and idiosyncratic as if Ruiz had engineered them all on his own.

Petit manuel d'histoire de France, for example, took the typical "Great Moments in History" television documentary and stood its conventions on their ear. To begin with, its narration was delivered entirely by children. Then there's the casting; the same actor would sometimes be seen in many different roles—making quite individual personalities appear part of some vast ensemble (which in terms of historical cliche they are). In other cases, numerous performers would be used in a single role, such as one bit in which five different actresses playing Joan of Arc at various times in her life come and go across the screen in relay-race fashion.

More revealing still is **Des grands événements et des gens ordinaires**, a documentary assignment that came about when Ruiz was asked to do a film about the national elections. Feeling, as an outsider, uncomfortable about tackling the problem as a whole, Ruiz suggested that he examine the issue from the point of view of the people in his own neighborhood. This in turn became a film about its own making. Doubt after doubt is raised about Ruiz's right to ask questions and of whom. Ruiz finally turns his attention toward the Third World, the one area he feels questions might more easily be directed by someone such as himself "because we are more powerful there." Ruiz's sardonic aside serves to underscore the way that filmmaking—particularly that of documentaries—involves an exercise in power, generally that of one class or social group (the filmmaker) over another (the subject being filmed). Moullet touches on this in **Genèse d'un repas** (a film edited, perhaps not coincidentally, by Ruiz's wife Valeria Sarmiento), as does Rouch in **Petit à petit**. Ruiz, however, isn't interested in stopping at mere satirical prodding, going on in later works to underscore (and undermine) the entire notion of authoritarianism all aesthetics are heir to.

The target that seemed the most logical to Ruiz was the Church, "the meta-institution, since its mission was to change the world and to the extent that it succeeded we are no longer conscious of its total impact.... I remember from childhood that the worst sin, far worse than murder or fornication was not to attend mass."* Ruiz was thus the ideal person to adapt novelist Pierre Klossowski's bizarre fantasy of religious intrigue **La Vocation suspendue** to television. Transposing its tale of a cryptic manuscript's disclosures concerning a strange religious sect within the Catholic church into a film about a cryptic *film* concerning the same subject, begun and abandoned by successive parties, Ruiz fashioned a labyrinth of narrative interchanges in which the authority of religion is put to the test. Power proceeds from acolytes' ability to engage in or resist the overall theological pull—here likened to the solution to a detective mystery thriller à la Poe's *The Purloined Letter*.

Ruiz went on from this to another Klossowski-related project, **L'Hypothèse du tableau vole**, also a telefilm but one that established what has become his new career, as far as international film circles are concerned. The work began as a straightforward documentary of Klossowski and his working methods, paying particular attention to the role played by painting both as a source of inspiration and as a formal subject. Ruiz's attention, however, soon moved away from this cut-and-dried approach to another inspired by Klossowski's novel *Le Baphomet*. The form the project eventually took was that of a standard television documentary with an unseen narrator introducing an unnamed collector (played by Jean Rougeul, Guido's critic/collaborator in **8½**) who takes us on what begins as a tour of his collection of works by a painter named Tonnerre. But standard educational film aspects are rapidly thrown out the window as the collector fills us in on the details of a mystery surrounding seven of the Tonnerre works in his possession. Evidently part of a series, one of them was stolen in the wake of a "scandal," the nature of which the collector is hazy about as he is not sure of its basis himself. As he tries to explain its meaning, the collector wanders through a series of rooms in a large mansion in which people stand about in *tableaux vivants* of the Tonnerre works. Pointing out specific details in best art history lecture fashion, the collector advances various theories about the meaning behind the paintings (salon confections brimming over with suggestions of sex and violence remindful of certain works of David and De la Tour with odd touches out of Balthus and Dali) and the curious gestures and postures of the figures within them. A digression to a discussion of a novel reportedly

---

Afterimage interview.

inspired by the "scandal" leads to rooms in which its events are shown in *tableaux vivant* fashion (this time suggesting a dime novel of the "Harry Dickson" variety). But no sooner has the collector come to a conclusion and advanced his theory that the gestures in the paintings are somehow linked together as signs of some religious ceremony, than he rejects it as too schematic. Wracked with doubt he wanders pensively about the rooms now overflowing with living-statue figures in *tableaux* that seem to bleed from one into another in ceaseless profusion.

On one level Ruiz's film is simply an entertaining satire of television conventions with a *soupçon* of mystery parody for good measure. But on another level this seeming lark raises entirely serious questions about the meaning and purpose of interpretation as it's generally received in western culture. Just as Tonnerre may have been at the service of forces (perhaps unconscious) far in advance of him, so Ruiz has put himself at the disposal of the *cine-roman* detective story. The collector's doubts are similar in tone to that of the narrator in **Des grands événements**. At the same time, however, there is a sense in which we, like the collector, should throw such a connecting link away as too schematic, for what Ruiz hints at throughout **L'Hypothèse** is a means by which he might vanish into his own *mise en scène*.

L'Hypothèse is very much the work of a cinematographer—in this case Alain Resnais's frequent collaborator Sacha Vierny. Shot in delicately shaded black and white, the film itself appears as much an object as the paintings it is ostensibly studying. As Vierny's camera moves through each painting-inhabited room in the film's finale, the ending of **Citizen Kane** is inevitably called to mind. **L'Hypothèse** as a whole, however, evokes another Welles work, **F for Fake**—also a film about paintings and their meaning. Just as **Kane** established Welles as a first-person voice in the cinema (the most important since those of the silent era), so did **F for Fake** question it—Welles disappearing behind the shadow of documentary filmmaker François Richenbach on whose work **F for Fake** was largely based. Ruiz finds another hide-and-seek game for authorial presence in **L'Hypothèse**. It is a film made to be lost in the maze of television—seen once or twice, remembered by some, forgotten by most. Select cinemas might be moved to give it a theatrical run, but on the whole it remains what it is—a film designed to be mistaken for that which it parodies (art history documentary). Released more widely, **L'Hypothèse** might have gained for Ruiz the fame won by Peter Greenaway for his **The Draughtsman's Contract** (1982), a film whose visual/allegorical concerns are so similar to those of Ruiz as to suggest the latter's direct influence. (One of Ruiz's *tableaux* figures even blinks in close-up like Greenaway's living statue.)

But Ruiz was soon off on another series of television tacks, turning out shorts on art exhibitions (**Pages d'un catalogue**, **Fahlström**), political debates (**Image du débat**), and even visual games (his **Teletest** providing a narrative palindrome of a couple either rising in the morning and going out, or coming home at night and retiring, depending on which direction the images are "read").

Where this constant expenditure (and dispersal) of energy was leading might best be seen in relation to **Les Trois couronnes du Matelot**, a relatively recent theatrical feature cheaply and quickly thrown together (like all Ruiz works) with financing partly provided through television. A kind of surrealist shaggy dog story about a mysterious sailor and his travels throughout the

Les Trois couronnes du
Matelot, by Raul Ruiz.
photo: Francois Ede.

world, Ruiz's film is a pastiche of nearly every seafaring adventure saga from Melville to Conrad, with bits of Poe's *Arthur Gordon Pym* and Isak Dinesen (the *Immortal Story* Welles used as a basis for a film of his own) tossed in for good measure. Replete with mysterious women (bodybuilder Lisa Lyon, no less), foretold curses, phantom ships à la the Flying Dutchman, and other fictional extravagances, **Les Trois couronnes** would appear to have no real meaning or purpose. Shot by Sacha Vierny in brilliant color, the film has no performances to speak of, its main energy being derived instead from the dizzying array of baroque compositions used to display its often outrageous actions (a prostitute in a room filled with dolls with brightly twinkling eyes, an unaccountably weird scene in which sailors are shown excreting worms from the surface of their skin). Wide-angle lenses are frequently used with camera angles that rival Carol Reed and Sidney J. Furie in their sheer unlikeliness. Objects of no apparent significance to the action (bottles, glasses, shoes, lamps, and whatnot) are frequently thrust into the left or right of the frame. Occasionally the screen takes on the look of a comic strip as in one sequence in which two figures who are the presumed center of the action are seen conversing prominently in the foreground of one shot only to be thrust into the extreme background of the next, which is dominated by a huge hand holding a cigarette. In another similar scene a temptress's furious cha-cha (the luscious Lisa Lyon giving it all she's got) is shown *through* a whiskey glass someone (perhaps the protagonist, perhaps not) is holding in the foreground. Weirder still are subjective shots in which characters who wear glasses are signified by glasses held before the lens—a mockery of the convention of the subjective p.o.v. concept.

Yet for all this giddy playfulness, there is a clear sense of Ruiz joking on the square in **Les Trois couronnes**. The sailor's travels are an obvious evocation of Ruiz's own sense of perpetual displacement. More important, in the film's climax political references of a less general nature come to the fore. The entire film is related in terms of a framing device in which the sailor tells a youth his life history. When he finishes the youth turns on him and savagely beats him to death—apologizing all the while for his behavior. "That part about the worms was really disgusting," the student proclaims, suddenly assuming the manner of a police official whose weary duty it is to torture and maim.

In his theoretical writings on the cinema, Ruiz has often spoken of the screen as a field in which "objects struggle to emerge from the background." In his view, "This constant tension, which makes abstraction impossible in the cinema, is like a subterranean current accompanying any series of images which, when it is applied to identical or similar objects as though these were traffic signs, follows a story which is half contained in the objects shown and half provided by us."[*] Ruiz cites the climax of **A Night at the Opera**, in which the backdrop for "Rigoletto" changes to a railway terminal to a ballpark to all manner of other locations, as an example of the way in which contextual shift alters meaning—something he sees as constantly operative in the cinema in ways the filmmaker, by and large, cannot control.

"When I was ten years old I saw *Flash Gordon* above all for its awkwardnesses, certain of which were truly poetic. One had more of a direct dialogue with the image and wasn't taken in. When I saw *Quo Vadis* for the first time it was something else...." Though delighted with this phenomenon, Ruiz is fully aware of its consequences in terms of the way cinema is made. "It's like a contract of mutual contempt. The manufacturer says one offers stupidity because the public is stupid. The public says everyone who makes films is an imbecile" (interview, *Positif*, #274). The challenge in Ruiz's eyes is finding ways to navigate this situation—to join the poetry of pop naiveté with his own sophistication. By working cheaply, quickly, and quasi-anonymously on projects that are by and large made to order, Ruiz puts himself in the position (from a production point of view) of an Edgar G. Ulmer. In point of fact, as "art" cinema has taken the place once occupied by the B film, Ruiz is certainly Ulmer's heir. The only difference is that, whereas Ulmer had a project to sell in some tangible manner,

---

[*]"Object Relations in the Cinema," *Afterimage* #10 (Autumn 1981), p. 87.

Ruiz—outside of the utilitarian context of television—has none. His **The Territory**, for example, appears cast in a commercial mode as its tale of a group of civilized adventurers forced by circumstance to turn to cannibalism plays right into the sub-genre made famous by the cheapie exploitation film **Survive**. Ruiz, however, is much more interested in cannibalism as an intellectual experience. The result was a film that, according to one of its investors—no less a B film eminence than Roger Corman—was "just not disgusting enough" for the horror market. That the cast and much of the crew of **The Territory** went off to make Wenders's **The State of Things**—a film whose subject is the difficulty certain films have in relating themselves to an ever-shrinking market—suggests the film had some purpose on another level. It is quite in keeping with Ruiz's ideas that the metaphor of cannibalism became a film which was cannibalized by another, so to speak.

In a way, the question of usefulness haunts the outer context of cinema more than it does Ruiz, who continues to work regardless. An example of this elegant indifference is his remarkable **Le Toit de la baleine** (*The Top of the Whale*). Shot (because it was financed there) in Holland, this 1982 feature is set in Patagonia, where an anthropologist and his wife (Jean Badin and Winecke Van Hammelroy) encounter the last surviving members of an obscure Indian tribe (Herbert Curiel and Ernie Navarro) overseen by a landowner and his mysterious aide (Fernando Bordea and Luis Mora). Repeated efforts at cracking the Indians' language have all come to naught. But as the anthropologist hero makes another try, the viewer encounters language problems as well. The film is in Dutch, French, Spanish, English, and German. Add to this the Indians' invented language and the result is a thoroughgoing sense of total cultural dislocation.

Shot in brilliantly inventive color by the great Henri Alekan (while actors are of little interest to Ruiz, cinematographers are of overwhelming import) largely in a single house, **Le Toit de la baleine** evokes such horror classics as **I Walked with a Zombie** and **Island of Lost Souls** as it wickedly parodies Werner Herzog's pathetic breast-beating exercises in cross-cultural empathy. The Indians are portrayed as what they are in culturally received terms—horror movie phantoms. Their possession of telepathic powers suggests a threat to their western visitors, who are as exploitative as their overseers (one of whom is described as a "communist millionaire"). The Indians get their revenge—clouding the minds of the others in short order (they begin to walk about like Dracula's handmaidens in no time at all). They are themselves, nonetheless, affected as well—sitting looking out the window in a scene toward the end the two argue over the relative merits of Beethoven and Mozart, one seen as having "nicer album covers" than the other.

Through it all, Ruiz's way with making the already peculiar seem even more so is everywhere evident as in his use of his leading lady's unfamiliarity with English. The long speeches he gives her in that tongue create an effect of "bad" acting at its most evocative (Maria Montez, the films of Edward

D. Wood, Jr.). "Are all proletariat strange?" the couple's child asks of the Indians. A strange creature as well, this offspring is of indeterminate sex. At one point he/she is seen ingesting rays of colored light—an event that brings about his/her (real? imagined?) pregnancy. "You shouldn't say such things," says the heroine of the child's increasingly poetic remarks. "People will believe you. Your metaphors will become a religion. And religion is the opiate of the masses."

For Ruiz, film is a form of anti-religion—a free zone capable of producing perpetual disbelief. There is no clear-cut audience for what is, for all intents and purposes, an anthropological Third World horror comedy. But toward whom **Le Toit de la baleine** might be directed is something Ruiz does not see as his problem. He is too busy making episodes for his television sci-fi series **Le Borgne**, or films like his surrealist children's adventure fantasy

Anne Alvaro in
La Ville des pirates,
by Raul Ruiz

La Ville des pirates. Then there's his adaptation of Racine's **Bérénice**, shot in a week with money advanced from a small French theater company. Filmed in black and white, it features more shadows than visible figures. "Expressionist cinema put at the use of Mexican melodrama," in Ruiz's words.

And then there are his other plans. A version of *Faust* with an all-vegetable cast, a *policier* for plants. They're all part of an overall project that might be said to link up on some other level whose meaning and purpose haven't as yet been disclosed. But then again they might not. They may all just be films like the others—*any* of the others (be they by Ruiz or Brakhage or even Norman Taurog). They go out into the world—the cosmos of our imaginations. They affect us. They are ignored. What remains is the force of cinema itself, an infernal machine that even now, in its present commercially dominated state of grotesque disproportion, continues to haunt our dreams.

. . . the argument thus far

If one common area of concern might be said to link the otherwise highly individual filmmakers discussed in the preceding section, it would be their willingness to engage with narrative processes. Whether partially or completely so involved, this one fact alone marks them as suspect in certain critical lights. The entire question of narrative's validity has been under heavy scrutiny for the past decade or so. Beginning in the early Seventies, politically informed theorists saw narrative as nothing more than an ideological weapon wielded by the status quo to keep its minions in line. Studies of what came to be known as Hollywood's "classic realist texts" (**Young Mr. Lincoln, Morocco, Touch of Evil**) stressed the gaps and omissions found in such works—seen in this context as desperate attempts to hide the true nature of the social fabric. High marks were awarded to filmmakers viewed as committed to the disengagement of narrative processes (Godard, Straub-Huillet, Oshima). Lacanian psychoanalysis added fuel to the fire now raging in opposition to anything smacking of fiction. The fact that current Hollywood cinema routinely sported gaps and omissions of Grand Canyon proportions, discontinuous semi-narratives that might be called Godardian if they weren't aimed at the mass market (e.g. **1941**) and shallow pretexts where characters used to be (**Indiana Jones and the Temple of Doom**) was conveniently ignored.

In the co-op avant-garde a similar process was at work as ranks closed around certain allegedly vanguard figures (need we mention them yet again?) leaving others less formally involved and more fiction-related to stand holding the critical booby prize as "transitional" figures pointing the way to the greater glory of those to follow (e.g. Jack Smith, Ken Jacobs). There was, to be sure, another side to this as well. The late Seventies saw what amounted to a creative backlash in the 8mm independent cinema that emerged from the rock club scene in New York. The members of this moviemaking "new wave" (e.g. Beth B and Scott B, Eric Mitchell, Vivienne Dick) saw no reason to apologize for their interest in character and incident. That some of them came to use this movement as a stepping-stone to a sort of semi-commercial "big time" (Amos Poe, Bette Gordon) is indicative of the fact that today the number of choices before American filmmakers has been sharply reduced. Some feel it is incumbent upon them to align themselves with one group or another. But, as Yvonne Rainer has shown, this need not be the case. Her position does show, however, that it takes a great deal of courage for any filmmaker to send his or her work out into the world without a guaranteed cultural context.

The filmmakers in the section that follows are all affected in one way or another by the contextual crisis outlined above. Some have embraced narrative; others have slid around its edges. Some have links to the co-op avant-garde; others are trying to find a new context in which independent work might be seen. All highlight important areas both new and old for the cinema to explore.

WARREN SONBERT.
Born in New York City, 1948.

>1966—*Amphetamine* (16mm, b&w, 9¼ min., sound-on-tape)
>*Where Did Our Love Go* (16mm, color, 15 min., sound-on-tape)
>*Hall of Mirrors* (16mm, color and b&w, 7¼ min.)
>1967—*The Tenth Legion* (16mm, color, 30 min., sound-on-tape)
>*Truth Serum* (16mm, color, 13½ min., silent)
>*Connection* (16mm, color, 13 min., sound-on-tape, two-screen projection)
>*The Bad and the Beautiful* (16mm, color, 32 min.)
>*Ted and Jessica* (16mm, color, 4 min., sound-on-tape, two-screen projection)
>1968—*Holiday* (16mm, color, 12 min., silent)
>1971—*Carriage Trade* (16mm, color and b&w, 61 min., silent)
>1975—*Rude Awakening* (16mm, color and b&w, 36 min., silent)
>1978—*Divided Loyalties* (16mm, color, 22 min., silent)
>1981—*Noblesse Oblige* (16mm, color, 25 min., silent)
>1983—*A Woman's Touch* (16mm, color, 23 min., silent)
>
>The films of Warren Sonbert are available from the Film-Makers' Cooperative, the American Federation of Arts, and the Museum of Modern Art Film Library.

The films of Warren Sonbert are something of an anomaly in the hothouse atmosphere of the American avant-garde. Colorful montages of people, places, and things, they would appear to have no particular aesthetic axes to grind—no great cosmic truths to sell. An almost childlike simplicity marks their matter-of-fact presentations of one clear, bright, easily readable image after another. Yet as these shots of city streets and country lanes, opera openings and fashion shows, flower stalls and flea markets pass in review, it becomes apparent—even to the least alert viewer—that an enormous amount of editorial wit and sophistication is involved.

We aren't meant to read these images shot on locations far and wide for their obvious content alone. Shape, color, mood, and movement are all part of the overall picture these often breathtaking individual views try to create. As they jump across the screen, freely mixing diverse locales, points of comparison with the work of Dziga Vertov immediately spring to mind. But the only party politics Sonbert sets forth are those of an alert, amused man of the world. There is no trace of snobbery in this (the title of Sonbert's magnum opus **Carriage Trade** is clearly ironic), just a simple desire to extend the class privilege of mobility as far as the camera can take it. This sense of cross-class generosity is matched by Sonbert's methodology. Each shot is brief. Close-ups are sparely used. We are never felt put upon to deal with any shot or sequence in a particular way. Ideogrammatic notions are advanced, but we are casually invited to disregard them if we wish. We can either engage ourselves with the material or disengage from it at any point— pay attention or turn indifferent to any shot or sequence we choose. We are, in short, in the presence of Roland Barthes's longed-for "image of a triumphant plural, unimpoverished by any constraint of representation ... a galaxy of signifiers, not a structure of signifieds ... the codes it mobilizes extend *as far as the eye can reach....* "*

Sonbert's story begins in the New York of the mid-Sixties, where serious-minded experiment and "Pop Art" irreverence freely and happily intermingled. His first film, **Amphetamine**, a study of teenage drug use set against the backdrop of the music of The Supremes ("Where Did Our Love Go?," "I Hear a Symphony"), is cast clearly in the mold of such avant-shockers as **Un Chien andalou** and **Fireworks**. Stark black-and-white interiors, where languid youths calmly insert needles into reed-thin arms, recall early Godard, while a bit of pure Hollywood glamour crops up in a lush 360-degree pan around two shirtless youths locked in a passionate embrace (a virtual remake of the climactic clinch between James Stewart and Kim Novak in Hitchcock's **Vertigo**).

Where Did Our Love Go, made the same year, takes a less immediately explosive route. A gaily colored Cook's Tour of a then-just-emerging demi-monde, it bops about the galleries, discos, shops, restaurants, and private parties where the young, hip, and urban congregate. A film of surface charm, a film *about* surface charm, **Where Did Our Love Go** nonetheless carries no small degree of moral impact. Comparing its visions of New York life to

---

*S/Z (New York: Hill & Wang, 1974), pp. 5-6.

those celebrated by Frank O'Hara in his poems, critic James Stoller percep-
tively called Sonbert's film "both a valentine and a farewell to a generation."*
This sense of casual but sharp social observation continued in the works
Sonbert began to turn out at an increasingly rapid rate throughout 1967.
The Tenth Legion, Truth Serum, Connection, and **The Bad and the Beautiful,**
like their predecessor, chronicle the lives of the city's trendy young moderns.
But while **Where Did Our Love Go** flips reflexively from one scene (in every
sense of the term) to another, these new works are highly organized affairs.

The Tenth Legion examines with an almost ethnographic rigor a landscape of fashionable apartments (the West Village), attractive jobs (teaching,
art collecting), and inviting pastimes (shopping, moviegoing). Sonbert had
by now developed a style of camera movement as elegant as his *soignée*
subjects—slow, decorous, hand-held tracks (**The Tenth Legion**), lush, brisk,
circular pans (**Truth Serum**), and a poised Hawks-style *plan américaine* to
anchor it all when still.

The Bad and the Beautiful is the apex of this period—a carefully staged
series of portraits of couples. Sonbert's subjects pose, mug, lounge about
languidly, and nuzzle one another with sexy abandon, hamming it up to
the hilt. All just fashionable larking about on the surface. But if these were
mere "homemovies," then they were the most *deluxe* sort ever made. Sonbert's attention to decor and detail here is very much in keeping with that
of Minnelli, to whom he pays tribute in the title. There's a sobering aftertaste
to it all as well. This, more than any of Sonbert's other works, is a film of
its moment. Everyone appears on screen in idealized form—looking good,
oozing charm, comfortably ensconsed in chic digs. None of it was going
to last. Sonbert seems to sense that fact in the way his camera appears almost
to caress his subjects. His presence makes each duet a trio, and as he films
each couple in turn, the film takes on the aspect of a series of farewells.

As the Sixties came to a close, Sonbert moved on. **Holiday** was a first,
tentative step, his camera gradually beginning to leave the city and its people
and take in a bit more of the world at large. Sonbert began to travel, both
to the usual European watering holes and more offbeat locales. The images
he collected on trips to Nepal, Afghanistan, India, and Tunisia gradually
took shape as a film. In and of themselves the shots were lovely, but as
Sonbert put them together they took on an aspect of something more than
simple armchair amusement. Shots of canal boats in Venice, camel riders
in North Africa, the streets of midtown Manhattan, and remote mountain
streams somewhere in India were now seen all together in one enormous
work. Through editing Sonbert had moved from an observer to a participant.
The Sixties social butterfly was now gone, and in its place a most industrious
caterpillar slowly wended its way through a maze of image/ideas first referred

---

*"Shooting Up," in *The New American Cinema: A Critical Anthology,* ed. Gregory Battcock
(New York: Dutton, 1967), p. 180.

to as *Autosalvage* and then, in turn through a four-year gestation, as *The Tuxedo Theatre, Tonight and Every Night*, the non-title *Footage from 1967-1970*, until finally settling down as **Carriage Trade** in 1971.

With **Carriage Trade** Sonbert hadn't simply taken a new turn in his career, he'd come to a complete halt and started all over again, from scratch. All his past works were now placed firmly behind him. The pop music soundtracks he'd used before were dropped in favor of complete silence. He even went so far as to take aspects of his old work and rework them into his new one. Images taken from **The Tenth Legion**, **Truth Serum**, and even **The Bad and the Beautiful** crop up in **Carriage Trade**'s international visual stew.

The plain and simple fact was that Sonbert had begun to take himself very seriously—as well he might, considering the implications of what he was now up to. The new film was like a vast cryptogram—an endless game of visual hide-and-seek. The sense of a subjective point of view common to avant-garde film (in this context the work of Jonas Mekas is especially comparable) doesn't function here. Sometimes Sonbert appears *present* in the action—pointing to a specific thing or action—at other times he seems completely removed, a mere recording device. The viewer, meanwhile, is extremely active, having to sort his or her way through this profusion of impressions. (Sonbert's double-screen films, **Connection** and **Ted and Jessica**, also offered great numbers of images at a fairly rapid rate, but without the sense of organization and control of his later works.)

In a lecture at the San Francisco Art Institute in 1979 (reprinted in *Film Culture* #70-71, 1983), Sonbert outlined some of what he was aiming for with all of this, using the opening sequence from his film **Divided Loyalties** as an example. The first shot is of a man seated in a cafe whom Sonbert describes as a "witty, urbane solo person." Next we see a bridge that suddenly "wavers, crumples, disintegrates." For Sonbert, the next logical step would be to show an image of "construction or planning," either "workmen building a house," or "people having a discussion." In the finished film the shots flash by in a few seconds. Even the most aware viewer would have a hard time sorting out the impression Sonbert outlines immediately. Still, this three-shot motif is there if only to be *sensed* on some subliminal level. The creation/destruction/regeneration motif continues throughout the film, on a thematic level Sonbert describes as "art vs. industry and their various crossovers." The numerous shots of construction sites and spectacles (the opera, the circus) that dot the work make this obvious. But the viewer's role in dealing with this isn't that of a passive receiver of predigested impressions—a fact Sonbert makes clear from his other comments in the same lecture concerning the filmmakers he admires.

To Sonbert, Brakhage is a "hero," the man who "liberated" film. "He suggested that all budding film-makers take an icepick to their lens to destroy Renaissance perspective," Sonbert recalled admiringly. But Sonbert wasn't about to do such a thing in his own work, which is very much Renaissance-based. His main models in this regard aren't avant-gardists but rather those celebrated Hollywood craftsmen Alfred Hitchcock and Douglas Sirk. From the former Sonbert claims his knowledge of "film vocabulary and form," as well as what he describes as a healthy mistrust of the "capitalist mentality." From Sirk (whom Sonbert feels is the most subversive talent ever to work within the studio system) there was the "purposeful flatness of his images" to appreciate, and the remarkable amount of visual tension they produced, especially in relation to figures and backgrounds. By contrast, Eisenstein, whose editing ideas some might think Sonbert would find of great interest, is regarded by the filmmaker with scathing disapproval. To Sonbert it isn't simply that Eisenstein's editing sees the world solely in terms of what he calls "all black or white" (Sonbert is no more fond of the cut from Kerensky to the peacock in **October** than are most film scholars), but that he disregards "compositional spaces. It's all up front—meaning is all contained in the foregrounds, with receding, weak, unplayed backgrounds."

It is this fore- and background tension that forms the crux of Sonbert's project and the viewer's specifically encouraged participation. Visual tension proceeds not merely from one shot to the next but within the shots themselves. Sonbert sets up a network of possible interchanges wherein themes are stated (e.g. art vs. industry) and motifs contrived (e.g. the three-shot pattern from **Divided Loyalties**). The regulation of all this foreground/background functioning is attendant upon the individual viewer's awareness.

Divided Loyalties, by Warren Sonbert. Still courtesy The American Federation of Arts.

There is no way of knowing what specific shot will capture the eye at any given point. Moreover, there is no way of knowing what *within* the shot will anchor that view. We are completely, utterly, free.

The views Sonbert provides are always simple, without visual distortions of any kind. Still, the viewer is never misled into regarding the camera's function as that of a window looking out onto some otherwise untouched "reality." Though what we see has sometimes been captured on the run (**Noblesse Oblige** has many quasi-reportorial sequences, such as one involving events in San Francisco in the wake of the assassinations of Mayor George Moscone and supervisor Harvey Milk), Sonbert doesn't shirk from *directing* his figures (they can't quite be called actors) much as does a Hollywood artisan. Shots are often framed to emphasize artifice—a street corner apes a theater stage, a fashion-show runway takes on the look of a salon painting. What matters is the integrity of individual cinematic moments. To quote Barthes again—this time apropos Sonbert's *bête noire* Eisenstein: "No image is boring, you are not obliged to wait for the next to understand and be delighted."*

For the past 18 years, understanding and delight have unfolded for Sonbert and his public along the usual avant-garde channels—museums, film clubs, and the like—even though the suspicion persists that they'd be just as welcome if placed before a mass public. That public may see Sonbert yet—if the project he has planned for the future comes to fruition. He wants to do a film of Richard Strauss's opera *Capriccio*—or to be more precise, he wants to do a film *contextualizing* that work. The setting will be the opera's world premiere, which took place in Germany at the time of the Third Reich. Sonbert plans to film, not the work in its entirety, but rather healthy selections from the opera set against the backdrop of that first performance. We'll see action unfolding not only onstage but backstage (intrigues among the cast members) and in the audience where (shades of **The Man Who Knew Too Much**) an assassination attempt on a top Nazi official is brewing. To complicate matters even further, Sonbert is planning to include a section—the details of which are at this writing still being sketched out—set in present-day New York.

The entire conception is, of course, ambitious in the extreme and—given the fact that Sonbert has never directed what is commonly referred to as a "major motion picture"—somewhat utopian as well. In terms of Sonbert's past work it's easy to see what he's up to here, with a foreground/background tension more marked than ever before. The fact of this marking will probably involve some degree of loss of spectator freedom as far as interpretation is concerned. There is little ambiguity in a situation in which high-minded aesthetic ideas (Strauss's musings on whether the words or the music come first in a work of art) are contrasted with a society coming apart at the seams. Sonbert hasn't avoided social comment in the past (e.g. **Noblesse Oblige**, certain moments in **Divided Loyalties** centering on homosexual life in San Francisco), but here he's jumping in feet first, placing himself

---

*"The Third Sense," in *Image/Music/Text* (New York: Hill & Wang, 1976), p. 52.

right on the line. The editing opportunities provided by the opera setting are infinite, with point-of-view shots for specific characters and frames within frames (i.e. the relation between stage space and backstage and audience space) offering ample room for visual play. But what most marks a project of this kind is the fact that it will push Sonbert (like Bruce Conner with his gospel film) across certain well-established lines. It is a risk very much worth taking.

 CURT McDOWELL.
Born in Indiana, 1945.

1970—*A Visit to Indiana* (16mm, color, 10 min.)
1971—*Tasteless Trilogy* (16mm, b&w, 16 min.)
    Wieners and Buns Musical (16mm, b&w, 16 min.)
    Confessions (16mm, b&w, 16 min.)
1972—*Ainslie Trailer* (16mm, b&w, 3 min.)
    Kathleen Trailer (16mm, b&w, 3 min.)
    Truth for Ruth (16mm, b&w, 4 min.)
    Peed into the Wind (16mm, b&w, 60 min.)
    Ronnie (16mm, b&w, 7 min.)
    Nozy Tozy (16mm, color, 5 min.)
    Siamese Twin Pinheads (16mm, b&w, 6 min.)
1973—*Dora Myrtle* (16mm, b&w, 13 min.)
    Boggy Depot (16mm, b&w, 17 min.)
1974—*Naughty Words* (16mm, b&w, 3 min.)
    Stinkybutt (16mm, b&w, 4 min.)
    Beaver Fever (16mm, b&w, 25 min.)
    Edwina Marlow (16mm, b&w, 12 min.)
    Fly Me to the Moon (16mm, b&w, 7 min.)
    I Suck Your Flesh (16mm, b&w, 20 min.)
    A Night with Gilda Peck (16mm, color, 20 min.)
    Pornografollies (16mm, b&w, 17 min.)
    True Blue and Dreamy (16mm, b&w, 17 min.)
    Nudes: A Sketchbook (16mm, b&w, 30 min.)
1975—*Thundercrack* (16mm, b&w, 120 min. and 158 min.)
1980—*Loads* (16mm, b&w, 22 min.)
1981—*Taboo: The Single and the LP* (16mm, b&w, 22 min.)
1983—*Stand By* (16mm, b&w, 60 min.)
1984—*Sparkle's Tavern* (16mm, b&w, 90 min.)
in progress:
    Initiation on King Street

The films of Curt McDowell are available from the Canyon Cinema Cooperative.

Curt McDowell is an entirely isolated figure on the American independent film scene. His largely sketch-like, black-and-white 16mm works, rarely over 30 minutes long, are as intimate and idiosyncratic as any in the avant-garde canon. But indifference to matters messianic and phenomenological has marked McDowell's as a talent destined to be ignored by the avant-academic cabal. Filled with raucous humor, virtually obsessed with sexuality, his films can't be said to lack what's commonly known as "commercial potential." But to judge from his sole semi-success in that area, **Thundercrack**, contextual problems crop up as well.

Written by filmmaker-actor (and McDowell mentor) George Kuchar, **Thundercrack** is McDowell's best-known work. A spirited mixture of sexual shennanigans and melodramatic spoofery, it appears cast in the fringe cinema mold of shock humor pioneered by John Waters—but there are several telling differences. Set in an "Old Dark House" on a "dark and stormy night," it features any number of explicit comminglings interspersed with long Tennessee Williams-like monologues by the establishment's owner, a cheerfully demented *grand dame* played with great style by a remarkable actress named Marion Eaton. Eaton's performance and the film's lush lighting

Marion Eaton in *Sparkle's Tavern*, by Curt McDowell

effects (Sternberg-style chiaroscuro dominates every scene) immediately place **Thundercrack** on a far more professional plane than the midnight movie norm. More divergent still, however, are the film's sexual dealings. **Thundercrack** is unashamedly, blatantly, bisexual. Every manner of physical commingling receives equal screen time, which has been known to disconcert more than one allegedly "liberated" fringe film spectator—leading to **Thundercrack**'s spotty history on that circuit. It has never received the across-the-board acceptance of a **Pink Flamingos** or **Rocky Horror Picture Show**.

Thundercrack's detailed plot and characterization place it at some remove from McDowell's other works, but the sense of upset it provokes in certain spectators is in many ways central to the filmmaker's concerns. Not that McDowell simply, childishly, wishes to cause upset. Rather, a real interest in exploring the root causes of our fears—and the way they're inextricably linked to our desires—marks McDowell's many, varied works. And to this end McDowell has never shown any compunction about putting his own situation on the line.

Two of his earliest works, **A Visit to Indiana** and **Confessions**, hone in on this self-analytical aspect, forming a diptych of sorts in the process. In the first film, McDowell takes 8mm homemovies of his hometown (placid color views of streets and houses blown up to a grainy 16mm) and sets them against the backdrop of an off-screen telephone conversation. A somewhat mysterious "old friend of the family" has called McDowell at his home in San Francisco to ask about how he's been doing since he left the family circle. The talk is cordial but distinctly edgy. The caller's voice drips with almost cryptic insinuations about the past. McDowell is very reserved, offering no real information about himself. Putting two and two together the viewer/listener can easily understand the situation. McDowell is the typical small-town boy who never "fit in" and consequently took off for the big city and its bohemian charms. Now confronted with his past he clams up. What McDowell is holding back comes bursting through in a great rush in **Confessions**.

This film's core is a simple medium close-up of McDowell lying on his bed in his apartment, the camera suspended above him at a slight angle. Speaking directly into it, he addresses his remarks to his parents, telling them of long-hidden secrets involving everything from childhood fibs and petty thefts to the fact that "I've been in love several times and only one of those times was it with a woman." McDowell is visibly upset over all of this—breaking down and crying as he tells each truth in turn. But what we're seeing here isn't a simple documentary, as the surrounding footage McDowell provides for this shot makes clear.

Confessions opens and closes with shots of George Kuchar crawling burglar-like in and out of McDowell's apartment window. In between servings of first-person candor (though filmed in one continuous take, McDowell's remarks are cut up into separate sections) we see shots of McDowell starlet Ainslie Pryor leaping about her room in speeded-up motion to the strains of an oddly up-tempo version of "I'm Confessin' That I Love You." How McDowell's words relate to these fragments isn't apparent on a linear level, but in terms of the film as a whole they place a fictional bracket around the reality of his speech. Just as the homemovie footage in **A Visit to Indiana** provided a frame of reference for its soundtrack (just as the conversation leads nowhere, the images are empty, meaningless), so here incongruous interruptions promise a dramatization that never takes place.

McDowell's discovery of personal extents and limitations through film began not long after his arrival in San Francisco in 1965. He had come to study painting at the Art Institute, but when he heard filmmaker Robert Nelson (**Bleu Shut, The Great Blondino**) give an address he changed his mind: "He made it all seem so easy. It seemed as if everything I wanted to do in the arts—drama, painting, music—could be done on film."*
McDowell received more encouragement along this line when he met and took up film study with George Kuchar. To Kuchar, who with his twin brother Mike had been turning out hommage/parodies of Hollywood melo-dramas since he was a teenager, film was an absolutely free field involving anything and everything. The only limitations were monetary or technical, which was another way of saying that the only limitations derived from the filmmaker's level of ingenuity and commitment. McDowell received help along these lines when he met Ainslie Pryor—"She wanted to act. I wanted to direct. Fortunately for both of us she had money." Pryor provided backing for a number of McDowell's initial efforts, many of which involved the slimmest of ideas. **Fly Me to the Moon**, for example, consisted of McDowell interviewing Pryor appearing in the guise of an already established Holly-wood star.

There was a deeper aspect to all of this play/pretend nonsense, however, for in working on a purely intuitive basis McDowell was beginning to delve into truly uncharted regions. **Siamese Twin Pinheads** is a prime example of this. Shot in a flat, frontal, pre-Griffith style, it presents the title characters played by McDowell and frequent collaborator Mark Ellinger in a starkly theatrical framework—introduced by a nun (Ellinger's sister Janey) as if part of a school pageant. No attempt is made to disguise the backyard skit nature of the enterprise. The "nun's" habit is made up of a long black skirt and a pea coat tossed informally over the player's head. The "twins" are likewise joined at the head by a piece of old stocking. Cheerily chirping about the progress the two have made since birth, the "nun" calls them before the camera to sing. Clad in diapers, the pair warble a croaky chorus of "Jesus Loves Me" while poking at their genitals in a distracted manner. After a brief blackout/pause, "sister" returns to announce that time has passed and with it the "Twins'" act has improved. The "improvements" seen in this second chorus of the song are McDowell and Ellinger's evident discovery of the joys of mutual masturbation. Pounding away at one another enthusias-tically, they chant with manic glee.

The sheer infantilism of a work like this can't be emphasized enough. Still there's a weirdly primitive power to it all as well—not *all* that far from similar grade-school japes by the likes of Alfred Jarry and Jean Vigo. By itself, **Siamese Twin Pinheads** is little more than a minor giggle taken perhaps a bit too far. In the context of the other varied comedies (**Beaver Fever**,

---

*Interview with the author, *Los Angeles Herald Examiner*, February 24, 1980.

Boggy Depot) and fantasies (**Tasteless Trilogy, True Blue and Dreamy**) that McDowell was turning out at a very rapid rate in and around the same time, however, it was something slightly more. McDowell was beginning to approach screen sexuality in a new way.

Ronnie, made the same year as **Siamese Twin Pinheads**, is a terse documentary vignette revolving around the voice and body of a young street hustler. Barely seven minutes long, it displays this real-life character nude before the camera, striking narcissistic "macho" poses as he jabbers away on the soundtrack (recorded separately from the image) in a run-on, sing-song manner. He tells of meeting McDowell and being invited by the filmmaker back to his apartment for sex—and the making of this movie. What's most startling about the work outside of its personal candor and conceptual adroitness (by the time it runs its course it has also explained its methodology and meaning) is McDowell's matter-of-fact willingness to reveal the camera's seldom acknowledged power as a tool of seduction. One might say that there are two films in **Ronnie**—the one McDowell made for his own private purposes and the one that we see. The shocking fact is that these two films are one in the same.

The camera's ability to serve more than one function comes into play in a somewhat different manner in **Nudes: A Sketchbook**. A series of portraits of friends and acquaintances varying in length, style, and overall tone, this half-hour featurette moves from the humorous to the mildly erotic to the thoroughly explicit and back again with absolute ease. Without dialogue, the film makes use of natural noises (rain, dripping water, traffic) and music (a pop tune written in her honor for Ainslie Pryor's turn) as background. The visual foreground is dominated by McDowell's shifting relationships to his subject—sometimes cool and objective, sometimes deeply and personally involved. The problem for the viewer is to navigate a space between these different poles.

There are no problems in dealing with the film's comic episodes, such as its opening, which finds George Kuchar romping through a mountain stream in his underwear—a parody of "September Morn." Ainslie Pryor camping it up before her bathroom mirror while dressing to go out likewise needs no explanation. But this can't be said of another mysterious bit in which a young woman (Barbara Linevitch) sits in her bathtub and stares at McDowell's camera with an almost chilling calm. Something's going on here, but we can't really tell what it is.

The erotic energy that flits around the edges of these and other sequences bursts through to the surface in several plainly sexual scenes that pop up along the way without any sense of fuss or bother. Melinda McDowell (the filmmaker's sister) is shown enjoying an energetic tryst with a boyfriend. The filmmaker himself puts in his own sexual two cents in one bit where he reaches from behind the camera to grope Mark Ellinger (the latter perusing a *Playboy* all the while).

Mystery returns, however, in another sexual scene, a kind of erotic mini-drama that finds McDowell and his camera nestled on the back porch landing of his San Francisco apartment, peering out onto the street in front with a zoom lens. A young man in loose-fitting trousers (evidently making some sort of delivery to another house on the street) has been spotted by McDowell's lascivious camera eye. Sensing that he's being watched, but not really sure who's doing the watching, the figure begins to approach the camera area, walking into the alleyway. Not seeing the camera, he continues past it into a backyard area on the other side of the building. Suddenly he falls to the ground (a fainting spell? a blow to the head?). McDowell and his camera tiptoe in. His hands pull the youth's trousers down as the screen goes black.

A teasing little game is being played in this episode (the most obviously contrived in a film made up mostly of loose improvised scenes). The viewer's status as voyeur is being exposed and undermined by the *mise en scène*. Normally, that status is secure—the camera operating for the viewer's benefit alone, keeping a safe distance between spectator and spectacle and the moral implications of watching. Consequently, out of sheer habit the viewer identifies with the camera position offered at the start of the scene, seeing it as an omniscient pseudo-character whose vision is to be unproblematically shared. But as the action unfolds, this cozy sense of subjectivity is shown to have its limits. McDowell has an access to the scene that we don't, the possibility of direct intervention—just as in **Ronnie**, we're on the outside looking in.

This notion of vision as a barrier comes through even more strongly in **Loads**. A sequel of sorts to **Ronnie**, it features a series of sexual encounters between McDowell, his camera, and various men who have taken his fancy. As in the earlier work, the filmmaker would appear to be totally honest and aboveboard about the entire process. As we see these men strut back and forth across his apartment in various stages of undress and arousal (McDowell's appearances in the film are limited to a few stray shots of a hand or the back of his head) the filmmaker explains on the soundtrack the circumstances involved in each case (how he met them, what they were like, whether he saw them again, etc.). But this process of revelation is also one of concealment. The men we see peering at the camera are plainly not looking at us. McDowell attempts to make up for this, in a sense, by trying to explain the basis of his attraction to each of them. But as he does so his voice becomes increasingly strained and halting. He has become aroused at the spectacle of his own past desires. Caught up in its processes he cannot explain its meaning with any precision. Consequently, while we *see* everything, as far as understanding goes we're on our own. We must interpose our desires between McDowell's and his subject's.

The problems attendant on this process figure even more prominently in **Taboo: The Single and the LP**. His most ambitious (and most ambiguous)

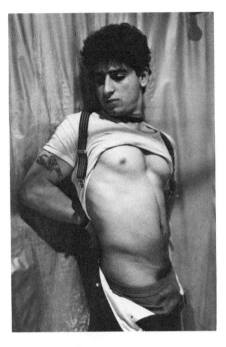

Fahed Martha in *Taboo: The Single and the LP,* by Curt McDowell

film to date, this mixture of documentary and psychodrama centers on McDowell's fascination with an Arab teenager named Fahed Martha. Though none of the film's action ever reaches a level of genuinely explicit sexuality, the anticipation of its doing so haunts the film's tense 22-minute running time. Fahed is shown in two settings: walking through a vacant lot with a friend (a neutral, almost idyllic backdrop) and by himself in McDowell's apartment. These sequences are the most sexually charged, as the muscular youth stands about posing before the camera, sometimes with shirt off or pants unbuttoned, never completely undressed. He appears to have assumed the function of an artist's model (which to some extent he was as McDowell, in addition to filming Fahed, has done a number of drawings and paintings of him). Just as the majority of the subjects in **Nudes**, Fahed is calm, almost serene—even when standing in McDowell's bathtub tied up with ropes like a martyred saint in a religious fresco.

Intercut with these scenes are others, with no apparent narrative connection, featuring George Kuchar, Marion Eaton, and other McDowell regulars. They are involved in what appears to be some sort of family quarrel—whispering to one another at first, and then breaking out in fits of pushing, shoving, and slapping around. What they're arguing over isn't made plain, for, like the other segments of **Taboo** (which feature natural sounds and music), this one has neither dialogue nor narration—just a few gasping and whispering noises.

Some long-repressed memory of McDowell's childhood is clearly being worked out in these scenes. Had he been more candid with his caller in **A Visit to Indiana**, this is what they might very well have talked about. Fahed's role in relation to this is more complex. It is as if McDowell were trying to graft his own personal history onto that of his object of highly fetishized affection—treating Fahed as a fully dimensional individual with a living history (the "real" scenes in the lot, the "fake" ones with the family) while maintaining (through the posing sessions) his object status all the while. Fahed, for his part, appears completely detached from the entire process as he stares at McDowell, and us. Like Bresson's "models" or Ophüls's **Lola Montes**, he is no more than a graphic presence—an empty center, a hook of flesh for desires not his own. He isn't transformed into a mystery figure (Dietrich in Sternberg, Karina in Godard, Kim Novak in **Vertigo**), which a full-blooded narrative would do to him. He is a fetish nonetheless, floating freely, mediated not by fiction but by possibility.

At a time when cinema's ability to fetishize is under psychoanalytic scrutiny, its voyeuristic potential viewed with approbation and horror, McDowell's films present more than a minor challenge. They are unremittingly honest—even to the point of revealing their own limitations. The view of voyeurism they offer may "deconstruct" its processes but while doing so increases its pleasures as well. Narrative is never central, but it isn't ignored either. Both **Sparkle's Tavern** and **Initiation on King Street**, two features begun in the late Seventies, are narratives concerning parent-child relationships. The first is a farce about, according to McDowell, "children hiding things from their parents and parents hiding things from their children." **King Street** is a poetic fantasy "about children and their parents meeting each other at the same age and experiencing each other's problems." Neither is sexually explicit in the manner of **Loads** or **Thundercrack**, but sex, as usual with McDowell, is involved.

It will be interesting to see what sort of space is allotted to these films on their release. Neither the increasingly jaded fringe circuit nor the artery-hardened avant-establishment is likely to leave out the welcome mat for them. But then McDowell, so obsessed with family relationships, has never shown ill-effects from his lack of a cultural home.

LIZZIE BORDEN.
Born in Birmingham, Michigan, 1950.

1976—*Regrouping* (16mm, b&w, 85 min.) Unavailable.
1983—*Born in Flames* (16mm, color, 90 min.) Distributed
    by First Run Features.

Like the political assassination that serves as a rallying point for its characters, Lizzie Borden's **Born in Flames** appears as if out of nowhere to provoke an otherwise moribund film scene. Years of dithering over formal procedures or (their mirror opposite) potentially attractive commercial compromise suddenly give way to the signal event of a film that is plainly and simply *about something*. Subjects generally repressed in America—race, class, feminism, social revolt, the power of the media—come tumbling out across the screen one after another with the liberating force of thought set free. There have been films made about all of the above ideas in the past (Godard's **Comment ça va**, Wajda's **Man of Marble**, and Yvonne Rainer's **Journeys from Berlin/1971**, to name only three), but few so dexterously and none so unintimidated by either the Scylla of theory or the Charybdis of the marketplace.

Reduced to its bare bones the film is disarmingly simple. Set in New York at some unspecified time in the future, **Born in Flames** deals with a series of events taking place within and without a number of feminist political groups attempting to take action in the face of growing societal decay. A so-called "Socialist-Democratic" government has been elected to office some 10 years earlier. But rather than provide change, this new power structure (apparently along the lines of Socialist governments presently operative in Europe) has simply taken up where the old one left off. Times are hard, jobs are scarce, and the minorities who are hoping to benefit most from the alleged political shift—blacks, Latins, and women—are in as bad a shape as ever.

For Adelaide Norris (Jeanne Satterfield), a leader in the Women's Army, an especially active minority coalition movement, the time for truly radical change has come. Encouraged by her political-activist mentor Zella Wylie (Flo Kennedy), Norris takes off on a secret mission to secure arms from a revolutionary group currently battling for control of the Northern Sahara. On her return to the United States Norris is picked up by the authorities (who had been monitoring her movements for some time) and whisked off to jail. The next day it is announced in the press and on television that she took her own life while detained for questioning in her cell. Norris's allies know this story to be untrue, as do many other activists in groups otherwise out of sympathy with the Women's Army. Soon all join forces, taking over a television station to broadcast the truth. As the film concludes, a new spirit of cooperation has arisen between formerly divergent groups. Galvanized into taking action, they set about planning a number of revolutionary maneuvers.

The above summary, like all diegetic condensations, centers solely on the film's narrative progression. Analysis of the workings of that progression brings other more important audiovisual figures into play. **Born in Flames** is more than the story of one individual or group; it is a network of different *kinds* of imagery, and the "story" just extrapolated from it is indicative of only one level of possible meaning.

The backbone of this network is the images of two clandestine radio stations, and the announcers who speak for them. Radio Phoenix, embodied by a black woman called Honey (both on-screen and off), is a low-keyed, sweet-tempered, community service-oriented operation. Optimistic in its outlook (Honey's speeches emphasize self-help and positive thinking), it is informally allied with the aims of the Women's Army. Radio Regazza, on the other hand, incarnated in the person of a white punk named Isabel (Adele Bertei), is an entirely different affair. Constantly warning of political uprisings to come, it is scornful of other groups' actions—particularly those of the Women's Army—and questions their ability to rise to the challenge of the growing social crisis, while offering no real alternatives of their own.

Astride these poles of alternating media calm and media chaos stands the official voice and vision of television. The ultimate arbiter of all societal events, it presents the *status quo* version of things we see and hear about in other contexts in the film. The efforts of the Women's Army to combat rape with brigades of whistle-blowing women on bicycles—scaring off male attackers with the visual force of their presence—are described on TV as "a dangerous outbreak of vigilante activity." Protests by groups seeking jobs are likewise denounced as "illegal," a stand bolstered by paternalistic reminders that the government is doing all it can to remedy the situation.

Interposed between the film's ungrounded narrative scenes—particularly those related to Adelaide Norris's story—these bits of media mediation provide a frame of reference, points of contrast, and a motor for the action.

Adele Bertei in *Born in Flames*, by Lizzie Borden

Honey in *Born in Flames*, by Lizzie Borden

News of community affairs announced by Honey on Radio Phoenix pairs off with images of group meetings. Isabel's dire diatribes on Radio Regazza are likewise linked to scenes of oppression (women being harassed on subways, losing their jobs to men, etc.). As for the official media, its objective correlative is provided by scenes of government agents monitoring the various groups and individuals involved—with special prurient attention given to the fact that Adelaide Norris is not only a feminist activist but a lesbian to boot.

With each scene and shot delivered with utmost brevity, **Born in Flames** is completely utilitarian in design. Everything we see and hear is put before us to make its point so that the film can move on to the next. Part of the point being made, however, bears on the nature of each audiovisual fragment—whether it proceeds from an alternative or official media character, or is related to other story fragments dealing both with Adelaide Norris and the society at large. What is crystal clear in every instance is the fact that no scene, no shot is to be accepted passively, but they are to be *read* in turn. The viewer must differentiate between contrasting fictional registers in order to relate the parts to the whole. This isn't an unusual or arcane discipline—it is in fact absolutely necessary in making even so much as five minutes of average television viewing comprehensible. The problem is that television doesn't seek our comprehension but rather its opposite—our blind acceptance of everything it offers. We are required not to understand but to submit unquestioningly to its will. Borden, in trying to make clarity of such chaos, strikes through **Born in Flames** a cultural/political blow of no small significance.

The directness and honesty of **Born in Flames** may appear surprising in light of Borden's background. An art history major at Wellesley, she took up painting and sculpture in the hopes of actively pursuing that field. Coming to New York in the early Seventies, she began to write art criticism for *Artforum*. But with her growing involvement in the feminist movement, Borden found herself moving away from the world she had once wanted to be part of. Knowledge of art history, coupled with her commitment to social issues, altered her perspective on what she now regarded an "introverted, white-middle class" modernist form. As for filmmaking along such lines, she'd become equally unnerved by the fact that such works "could be so easily contained within the art world ... Paul Sharits and people like that being carried by Castelli-Sonnabend." Wanting to reach a different audience and work within a feminist context at the same time, Borden made her first feature, **Regrouping**.

A work Borden is now dissatisfied with (seen at a few film festivals and special screenings, it was never put into wide release), **Regrouping** is a study of feminist consciousness-raising sessions and the problems of power and manipulation Borden felt were attendant upon them. The film weaves actual footage of a group in action into a fictional context (thus casting doubt on the nature of the "truth" involved) through layers of voice-over narration—a process that raised the ire of members of the group involved. This particular learning experience was tied to other problems Borden feels faced the movement then as now. "I was very distraught coming to New York and living here a long time and finding that this group of feminists didn't deal with that group of feminists. And how many black women did I know? None. How many Latin women did I know? Class and race really did divide people, and just a *slightly* different political stance divided middle-class women."* **Born in Flames** grew out of that frustration. An attempt at imagining some event or circumstance that might unite these otherwise segregated forces in some way, the film almost inevitably pivots on the notion of armed struggle.

"I asked many women if they would ever use violence and the answer was always no," Borden noted. "How convenient for the government."† Not surprisingly, in terms of film spectacle this same violence provided **Born in Flames** with its singular cutting edge. The cinema is filled with images of armed men representing every possible political perspective. Similar images of women are rare. An isolated *film noir* femme fatale or two holds the trigger hand to be sure, but when it comes to women working together— particularly in a context where the possibility of an alliance with like-minded males is never considered—the results are quite different. Criticism from a number of quarters was aimed at **Born in Flames** for allegedly advocating violent action—the most noteworthy coming from archivist Tom Luddy and filmmaker Jean-Pierre Gorin, both allegedly appalled by what they perceived as Borden's "macho" attitude.

What's most revealing about these and other responses to **Born in Flames** is the light they shed on the status of representation. As a work of science fiction, Borden's film can't be said to advocate anything—but only to advance ideas. The actions shown are entirely imaginary, and in some instances (the bike brigade attack being a prime example) highly fanciful. The film is rife with dark ironic humor, both through line delivery (Adele Bertei's too-cool snarl, Flo Kennedy's delicious deadpan) and situation (such as a particularly striking montage of "women's work" including everything from secretarial duties, assembly line routines, wrapping poultry, and pulling a prophylactic onto a penis). Nothing here is to be seen or heard on a literal level.

Tied up with this is the fact that many of the situations and much of the rhetoric of **Born in Flames** refer pointedly to political events in the recent past, both in the United States (the so-called "Weather Underground") and in Europe (Adelaide Norris's death recalling the similar passings of the Baader-Meinhoff group members in Stammheim prison). Similarly striking is that everything we're seeing is taking place against the backdrop of a New York very much of the here and now. Borden makes no attempt to disguise this fact, as budgetary limitations prevented her from filling in the details of what such a future might be like à la **Blade Runner**. But this limitation is quickly transformed into an advantage. No reason not to connect a

---

*Interview with Lizzie Borden, *The Independent*, November 1983.
†Marcia Pally, "Is There a Revolution after the Revolution?," *The Village Voice* (November 15, 1983).

personality like Isabel with the punks of today or the chic women of the "Socialist Women's Alliance" with their modern Soho sisters. The result is a film that pulls in several directions at the same time—forcing us to see the past and the present commingling as things yet to come.

What this all serves to grate against is the fact that film, for many and far more varied audiences than might be expected, is a field of wish fulfillment. It is not only the shop girl who dreams, but the university professor with sights set on some all-encompassing Poundian paradigm for God, Art and Man, or the political radical searching the screen for some social solution he or she can't see in actual life. By asking more questions than she'll ever attempt to answer, bending the entire structure into an increasingly baroque series of "what ifs," Borden is an untenable figure to many.

In the limited venues independent films of its ilk are allotted in this country, **Born in Flames** has nonetheless made a substantial impression— respectful reviews, lively audience reactions. Borden, for her part, is pleased but far from fully satisfied, as the problems that inspired her to make the film have come to haunt its distribution: "It's wonderful that it was shown at the Film Forum in New York and got a good reaction. But how do you get black women into a theater like that?" Taking matters into her own hands Borden has been going around with the film herself, showing it to disparate groups to get their reactions.

By the time she completes her next project, a film about the business rather than the spectacle of prostitution, Borden may have some new answers to this pressing question. For the moment, with **Born in Flames** she has taken an all-important first step toward taking up audiovisual arms in what promises to be a prolonged struggle for the expansion of cinematic space.

 SALLY POTTER.
Born in London, 1950.

1968—*Jerk* (8mm, b&w, 5 min.)
1969—*Play* (16mm, b&w and color, 8 min., two-screen projection)
1971—*H'Ors d'oeuvres* (16mm, b&w and color, 10 min.)
1972—*Combines* (16mm, b&w and color, 20 min., three-screen projection)
1979—*Thriller* (16mm, b&w, 40 min.)
1983—*The Gold Diggers* (35mm, b&w, 90 min.)
None of Sally Potter's films are at this writing available in the United States. Inquiries should be made through the London Filmmakers Cooperative and the British Film Institute.

"Please, please, please give me back my pleasure, please give me back my good night out, please give me back my leisure time," a voice sings plaintively on the soundtrack of **The Gold Diggers** just prior to the film's opening credits. Not an unreasonable demand. The only problem stems from the sort of pleasure—the kind of "good night out"—involved. And that in turn turns on the question of who is doing the asking and why.

The voice on the soundtrack is that of the film's maker, Sally Potter. A member of the British avant-garde who has dared to venture beyond the co-op coterie, Potter has met with equal measures of acceptance and rejection for doing so. **Thriller,** her feminist reworking of Puccini's *La Bohéme,* met with immediate acclaim in the more adventurous film circles that have sprung up in both England and the United States over the past few years (not an organized movement at this point, just a nomadic band—a like-minded happy few open to both Snow and *Screen*). But unlike its predecessor, **The Gold Diggers** hasn't been so comfortably culturally ensconced. As a BFI production featuring a major star—Julie Christie—this experimental musical/adventure has suffered according to certain conventional critical lights in comparison with its immediate *production* predecessor—**The Draughtsman's Contract**.

The BFI's charter allows for the allocation of funds only to those film projects that otherwise might not have gotten them through ordinary commercial channels. This was doubtless the way Peter Greenaway's Regency period mystery thriller must have looked on paper, especially as regards its obsession with form and allegory. On the screen, however, a mixture of sex, violence, and upper-class backbiting made **The Draughtsman's Contract** a surefire box-office success. In fact, had it been known in advance that Greenaway would be so adept at directing performers in the accepted "art film" manner (Noel Coward cryptic with Pinter pauses for important points), mainstream producers would have surely overlooked his experimental past (dessicated neo-Framptonian exercises cataloging people struck by lightning or possessing names beginning with the letters F-A-L-L) and climbed aboard the gravy train.

The Gold Diggers boasts no such easy charm. On screen as on paper, it is a work that could only have been financed by an organization like the BFI. But once a precedent has been set it's hard to break out of—especially as far as the upper-middle class consumers **The Draughtsman's Contract** had attracted (moviegoers who wouldn't be caught dead at an avant-garde film) were concerned. With no conventional plot or (worse still) male characters of an attractive demeanor (or vide **The Draughtsman's Contract** an attractively unattractive demeanor), **The Gold Diggers** offers no pleasure—no "good night out"—whatsoever to these viewers. At its premiere at the BFI in May of 1984, it met with the sort of press hostility generally reserved for events on the order of Peter O'Toole's production of "Macbeth." There are, of course, many reasons that a film so light and sweet-spirited should be so reviled. The majority of them revolve around the criticism that Potter as a woman filmmaker in Britain (itself a rarity) was bound to receive on being granted major government funding for a feature film, regardless of its contents. But something more fundamental also is involved in the heat **The Gold Diggers** has taken, something that relates directly to Potter's notion of pleasure. For her, pleasures are of a subtle but nonetheless highly transgressive order—that of women taking power over cinematic space.

Sally Potter began in film in a mode commonly associated with the British avant-garde of the last two decades. **Jerk** consists of superimposed images of heads made up to form one composite, all-purpose face. **Play** places two images of two sets of twins, filmed simultaneously (one color, one black and white), next to one another, examining the interplay when the participants move between these different spaces. Multimedia presentations followed with **Combines**, a triple-screen work specifically designed to be shown with a dance performance. Dance and music became Potter's principal field in the late Seventies. With Jacky Lansley (an important player in **The Gold Diggers**), she formed the "Limited Dance Company," creating a number of solo and ensemble works with future film collaborator Rose English. During this period, she also worked with the women's music group "Fig," and set up a song-writing partnership with Lindsay Cooper (who wrote **The Gold Diggers**'s score). Consequently, when Potter returned to filmmaking with **Thriller** it was by a different door than the one she had originally entered.

From a point of aesthetic attack that compares quite felicitously with the work of choreographer-turned-filmmaker Yvonne Rainer, **Thriller** is unashamedly theatrical in design. In a barren, quintessentially urban loft space covered in an eerie half-light (suggestive of German expressionist cinema), a young black woman with short-cropped hair (Colette Laffont)—identified on the soundtrack as Mimi, the tragic heroine of Puccini's opera—moves through a series of *tableaux vivants* occasionally breaking into bits of dance movement. She is accompanied through most of these terse routines by performers representing the opera's heroes, Rudolpho and Marcello, and the *demimondaine* Musetta (played by Rose English). Intercut with stills of a standard production of the opera, this oddly pitched visualization would be aleatory in the extreme were it not for the soundtrack, which, in marked contrast to the images, is quite direct about the meaning it intends to convey. As a result, what would otherwise have been a loose network of images is forged aurally into a highly organized analytical program.

Mimi has come to the conclusion that her death in the opera's finale was a murder. Moving through what amounts to an artistic vision of limbo, she sets out, like any good detective, to examine the evidence in the case. But instead of the magnifying glass of yore, this sleuth turns to theoretical texts involving feminism and psychoanalysis. "She was searching for a theory that would explain her life—that would explain her death," the narration notes, "They had written the books; by reading them she hoped to understand."

Against this rarified backdrop, Potter's Mimi comes to the conclusion that the culprit involved was less an individual than an entire social order reflected in the opera that contains her. Mimi feels she died young because "an old seamstress would not be considered the proper subject for a love story." Likewise, while her death was tragic, its dramatic center is Rudolpho and Marcello, transformed into "heroes in the display of their grief." Most important of all, however, is the separation made in the opera between Mimi and Musetta, "the bad girl, the one that didn't die." Only by forging a relationship with her can Mimi break the virgin/whore dichotomy and thus destroy the cul-de-sac of the opera's plot.

If the above summary sounds as if it falls just slightly short of parody, it's not by accident. There is no denying the intensity of Potter's commitment to feminism or her respect for theory. But it doesn't also follow that she's unaware of the risk of ideological oversimplification in an undertaking of this kind. No modern viewer, regardless of socio-political stripe, needs to be reminded that the attitudes expressed by a work like La Bohéme are "old-fashioned" and "out of date." But just beneath this outmoded whole, stands a set of culturally perpetuated specifics—which is where the mystery underscored by Potter's title comes in. In questioning the irrationality of her death Mimi takes on the form of Marion Crane (Janet Leigh) in Hitchcock's **Psycho**, a Musetta/whore figure of the modern era, whose death is investigated by her sister Lila (Vera Miles), a Mimi/virgin figure. Potter refers to the Hitchcock film overtly in soundtrack quotations from Bernard Herrmann's score and in one scene/shot of Mimi laughing before a mirror, her hand cupped to her mouth—evoking Lila startled by her own reflection in the mirror during her climactic tour of the Bates mansion.

Mimi laughs in another important moment in **Thriller** as well—just after the narrator's speech about the role of theory in her investigation. She is reading a text by Julia Kristeva in the Tel Quel group's collection Theorie d'ensemble. Looking over a page or two, she suddenly bursts out in a fit of the giggles and drops the book to the floor. More than offhand ridicule is involved here. Potter is keenly aware of the distance such theory—however valid—has from actual practice.

At the same time, Mimi's laugh evokes another—Claudia Cardinale's in Fellini's 8½. In a scene depicting one of Guido's (Marcello Mastroianni's) fantasies, she is seen dressed in a white slip peering attentively at a book of art illustrations, her body locked in a classical ballet pose. Suddenly she shifts about, her arms collapsing between her legs, her head pulled downward then back up again, in an explosion of "vulgar" laughter. Claudia is, of course, a highly traditional image of woman's "mystery" as seen by men. Potter's Mimi is no less mysterious, but the context in which she resides doesn't allow for simple sexual objectification. Sitting on a barren wooden stool, posed before a mirror where she "waits for a clue," held aloft like a banner by the equally opaque Rudolpho and Marcello figures, she isn't recuperable as anyone's dream girl. Rather, she is simply a figure of a woman set against a field of images and ideas in which the fact of female social powerlessness is brought forth undisguised.

This oscillation between the obvious (the soundtrack) and the oblique (the images) reaches a climax of sorts in **Thriller**'s finale, which finds Mimi and Musetta in a gentle embrace while Rudolpho and Marcello climb out a window in the background. The soundtrack indicates some form of female solidarity has been achieved. The image, however, is subtler. The pose of the women could also be said to suggest the traditional view of suffering as woman's lot (e.g. Scarlet comforting Melanie in **Gone with the Wind**). *La Bohéme* being the sort of work it is, analysis can only indicate problems rather than offer broadbased solutions. And this is where **The Gold Diggers** comes in.

The theoretical specificity of **Thriller**'s narration is absent from this new work—save for the song quoted earlier and the (scarcely unanticipated) announcement by one of the film's two heroines that she is interested in "redressing the balance." The balance in question is that of the cinema itself, referred to in an equally straightforward manner in a riddle posed over the film's opening (post credit) shots. First come views of barren wintry landscapes (shot on location in Iceland in glittering black and white by cinematographer Babette Mangolte) inhabited on occasion by a solitary female figure. Then, as the film's score (delicate tinkling sounds with

The Gold Diggers, directed by Sally Potter

occasional notes of Prokofiev ominousness) rises on the soundtrack, we see an extreme long shot of a group of figures slowly wending their way up a glacier. No closer shot is needed to indicate that they are men—social and cinematic convention tells us that. As they move away from us the voices of two women (one clear and bell-like, the other with a marked French accent) rise on the soundtrack to join the music: "I am a beam of light. I move continuously. I am bigger than life, yet I do not breathe. You know me intimately, yet I know you not at all," and so on.

"We have 90 minutes to find one another," one of the voices remarks toward the end of this litany. But the union referred to isn't between them alone, but rather between spectator and spectacle. For what follows is less a narrative than a circulation of images and sounds moving against narrative's grain. At its center are two women, one of which—Julie Christie—we know intimately, the other—Colette Laffont—not at all. In a single action (which is in essence the only one of the entire film) they come together, setting the process that follows in motion.

Julie Christie is seen in Victorian-era costume at a lavish ball, waltzing with a series of men. Suddenly Colette Laffont enters on a horse, sweeps Christie up onto it and rides off. This sudden interruption is quickly revealed a violation of cinematic space, destructive not simply of realism, but of the ideological imperatives that give realism its force of import. Colette Laffont's character, Celeste, is a modern office worker. Julie Christie's character, Ruby, is a classical heroine figure (like Mimi) with no occupation other than the maintenance of her own beauty and desirability. Obviously these women have nothing to do with one another in the cinema—as it's presently constituted.

Celeste wants to find out "what's behind" the numbers she's been copying from one computer column to another in her job. Ruby wants to understand a past she has forgotten because "those were the terms of my existence." So far, so obvious, with modern heroine posed against classical one—except for the background against which Potter places these twin quests. It is, for the most part, a city at night—dark and rather ominous, inhabited only by the heroines and groups of comically sinister men (much on the order of Rudolpho and Marcello in **Thriller**) in constant comic pursuit of them. The daylight shots are of Iceland, seen in one sense as some sort of forgotten landscape where an alternate scenario might be enacted, and in another sense as the land of Ruby's memory—where an almost idyllic relationship with her mother was somehow left abandoned.

Ruby discovers an inkling of something else related to her past in a scene backstage at a theater where she meets a dancer (Jacky Lansley) running through a new routine. As she taps and twirls about, the dancer tells Ruby that things have become more difficult for her "since I stopped working with a partner." Now whenever she meets the audience's gaze "I forget my steps." Ruby wants to help her out but is almost immediately

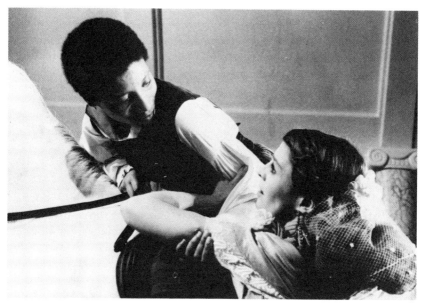

Colette Laffont and Julie Christie in *The Gold Diggers*, directed by Sally Potter

grabbed by a stage manager who thrusts her—without preparation—before an audience in a play set in the frozen North of her memory.

Celeste meanwhile has been wandering through the corridors of power—represented by an ultra-Kafkaesque "Expert" and his assistant. In a room dominated by an enormous desk they tell her how capitalism began ("One man gave a banknote to another man") with gold serving as both a representation of its "integrity" and a social ideal of "perfection." This in turn folds into the film's climactic image of gold and women in ceaseless circulation in a quasi-Masonic ceremony. Ruby, costumed like a queen, is carried on a throne by one group of men alongside another group of men carrying a stack of gold bars. "To the bank with the Beauty, to the bank with the gold. Both make money and neither grows old," they chant.

As in **Thriller** the finale of **The Gold Diggers**, which follows this scene, pivots on female solidarity. But the effect here is quite different. Solidarity between Ruby and Celeste has been present more or less from the start, following the horse rescue scene. Though Ruby's search is similar to Mimi's, no specific goal is attached to it. Celeste likewise has no ulterior motive behind her economic investigation, other than curiosity. But as the two run from the bankers and go into another, smaller theater, it's clear the situation has changed. Ruby sits in the audience as Celeste mounts a small stage to sing a song denouncing the status quo in brisk short order: "Plundering digging, impatient till they get their fill ... Old school ties, Commonwealth lies, May you crumble and sink!" We next see Ruby back at the ballroom as she was at the film's opening, laughing this time as she drops each of her dancing partners unceremoniously to the floor. The escape by horseback is repeated, this time as an expected event rather than a surprise, followed shortly afterward by a shot of the women swimming toward a boat being repaired by a woman welder. She greets them with an open, welcoming smile.

It is in the smile of this welder that the special kick (and for some the special irritation) of **The Gold Diggers** can best be perceived. She is a real person in a real job. She does not "belong" in this cinematic world, yet she is the point toward which the action is leading.

The path this action takes can quite easily be lined up and elucidated along the lines spelled out in the narration of **Thriller**. But there is another subtler way to examine Potter's achievement. For to go through **The Gold Diggers** in linear fashion is to risk joining together the areas the film tries to keep separate. There is no explanation of why the men are chasing Ruby and Celeste or of what they want from them. Though ridiculed, they're far from caricatured brutes, which in some ways makes them more untenable to certain souls (who would be quick to dissociate themselves from obviously reprehensible behavior). No information is given as to how they've managed to capture Ruby (or if they have in fact done so) in order to place her in their ceremony. No hint is offered as to how she escapes from them to run off with Celeste. The impossible leap of the opening horse escape episode is repeated again and again in scenes where only an enormous leap of faith can make possible the "sense" that ties one dramatic action to another.

What Potter offers in its place is evocation—image/ideas related not to others in the film but to other films, and the way we've viewed them. By opening **The Gold Diggers** at the BFI, Potter was given the opportunity to program a season of other works that put her film in historical context. Alongside such expected choices as **Lives of Performers**, **The Gold Rush**, **The Gold Diggers of 1933** (an important source for the Jacky Lansley scene), **The Trial**, **Doctor Zhivago**, and **Alexander Nevsky** (the Iceland scenes featuring Lindsay Cooper's music are a virtual hommage to the Eisenstein-Prokofiev classic) were other less expected entries. **The Lady Vanishes** was included because "the pursuer and pursued are women"; **The Red Shoes** because the heroine "must be 'owned' by one man ... her 'choice' is no choice." **Queen Christina** was chosen for its images of "female power and powerlessness"; **The Saragossa Manuscript** for its "circular structure"; and so forth in a list that also includes such interesting and suggestive choices as **Hellzapoppin**, Joyce Wieland's **Rat Life and Diet in North America**, and Alexander Kluge's **The Power of Emotion**.

All of this is good old-fashioned film aesthete fun, but there's a deadly sober aspect to all of it as well. Something from each and every one of these films can be glimpsed in an image—in a moment—from **The Gold**

Diggers. Seeing them all and then relating them to Potter's film is not the point. Rather, it is the way that each image/moment so connected asserts itself that the power of an alternate variety of cinematic imagination makes its voice heard. We have been traveling, after all, not through the main route of narrative, but along its fictional byways. This is what the characters in other films do while they're asleep. This is where they go when they leave the shot. The landscape they inhabit is inevitably dark and strange, for it's an unchartered region of desire—of pleasure—musing over what possible direction it may take, what form it might assume. This is no new thing in cinema. But there is a difference between a voice drifting across the screen from time to time (Chytilova's **Daisies**) or gradually swelling up from a background (the films of Marguerite Duras) and the one we hear here—formally announcing its desire to take control.

... the argument thus far

Segregation haunts the avant-garde. As if in fear of some force of contagion, lines (often as not quite arbitrary in nature) have been drawn again and again over the years, separating the commercial from the "personal," the narrative from the "structural," the political from the "visionary"—all in the name of distinguishing the "bad" from the "good." Curiously, those works of cinematic nonfiction usually referred to as "documentary" have been left out of this discriminatory process.

Some fully approved avant-garde talents have worked in this area from time to time—most notably Stan Brakhage in his "Pittsburgh" trilogy (**Deux ex, eyes, The Act of Seeing with One's Own Eyes**). But these studies of hospitals, police work, and autopsy procedures were regarded (inevitably) more in relation to their maker's history than that of their genre. Some of the figures dealt with in this volume (Bruce Conner, Luc Moullet, Werner Schroeter, Raul Ruiz, Warren Sonbert) have dealt with nonfiction material in one way or another. But theorizing how these (for want of a more precise term) fiction-oriented filmmakers might relate to the nonfiction arena pivots to no small degree on the way the genre has been traditionally regarded by the cinematic institution in its entirety.

The nonfiction film has always been viewed with a curious mixture of respect and indifference. Critics and scholars of all stripes have granted high marks to such figures as Robert Flaherty, Humphrey Jennings, and Jean Rouch—quite diverse talents. But questions pertaining to why such work, if so valued, has received only limited public exposure have rarely been addressed, much less answered. The main unacknowledged reason for this is the hold fiction in all its forms (both avant-garde and "commercial") has on the entire moviegoing process. We go to the cinema to escape, to dream. The nonfiction film's "reality" in this regard isn't appropriate image/idea fodder for the fantasy form viewer desire is expected to take. (This is one explanation of why rock documentaries like **Gimme Shelter** and **Woodstock** have, to date, been the only examples of the form to achieve some level of commercial viability. Fantasy is the life's breath of rock.) The *real* of nonfiction consequently threatens to take us back to rather than out of ourselves.

On another equally unhelpful level are critical perceptions of the cinema as a mere palimpsest behind which stands a complete, seamless, absolute reality (n.b. the writings of André Bazin and Siegfried Kracauer). Seen in this light, nonfiction filmmakers aren't praised for what they actually do, but rather for what they pretend *not* to. The best technical procedures are judged to be those that absent the filmmaker from the scene as much as possible, the better to let this reality "speak for itself." In recent years a number of theoretical salvos have been launched against this notion (the most important from Noël Burch, Stephen Heath, and Jean-Louis Commolli). But useful as they've been in clearing the cultural air, the unhappy by-product of such writing has been the downgrading of the entire nonfiction genre. Just because the "reality" of such films is no longer to be accepted as an unquestioned given is no reason to reject them out of hand as valueless. Logically, the critical context should simply shift to the ways in which these works have constructed the "real" either through editorial processes after the fact (e.g. **The Sorrow and the Pity, Le Chant du styrène**) or via the camera's intervention as a creative presence on the scene (**Primary, Chronicle of a Summer**).

But more than anything else, consideration of filmic nonfiction's ways and means on any level must come to grips with the role television has come to play in the process. Today almost all of television involves nonfiction material—from news and sports programs, to game shows, Johnny Carson, and even certain commercials. Distinguishing what is real from what is fantasticated in any of this is nearly impossible. Television absorbs everything it touches into one muddy all-encompassing image-flow. As a result, the relation of independent nonfiction work to television's ideological domination isn't one of a simple opposition of technical means and resources (as is the case with Hollywood in comparison to the avant-garde). Moreover, television has been all too eager to feature independent documentary work on its webs—as witnessed by the medium's ongoing romance with Frederick Wiseman. But this in turn inevitably raises the question of the precise *kind* of work the medium finds so laudable.

As their titles alone indicate (**Welfare, High School, Hospital, Model, The Store**), Wiseman's films supply completely predigested views of the worlds they present so glibly. Without narration or grounded narrative flow (the films rarely deal with individual personalities), they offer up select views of people and events fully in keeping with the class prejudices of the very particular public (the upper-middle classes) "public" television is intent on serving. Like "60 Minutes," Wiseman's films tip us off on the "inside story" of the subjects they presume to cover. But unlike that popular CBS program the insights offered are quite unsensational in nature. Mass education is boring (**High School**), high-pressure sales outfits are insidiously money-grubbing (**The Store**), fashion models are soulless vapid creatures devoid of personality (**Model**), and so on, and so forth. Far be it from Wiseman to advance one iota of information to undercut such dogma or (most important of all) analyze his ostensible subjects in any thoroughgoing way. All we see are surface effects, never what causes them. Were Wiseman to delve beneath this lacquer (to explain, for example, how a department store's operations reflect on the consumer society as a whole and the desire it caters to, or the societal hierarchy that places the *haute couture* Appollonia Von Ravenstein wears in one scene of **Model** on a different plane from the stockings she hawks in another) there is considerable reason to believe his television career would be at an end.

Seventeen, Joel DeMott and Jeff Kreines's study of adolescent race relations in the Midwest, was kept off the "public" airwaves it was initially designed for—largely as a result of the objections lodged by the Xerox Corporation, one of the corporate underwriters that keep "non-commercial" television in line. Corporate approval is synonymous with prime-time airing and advertising ballyhoo. Without it programs are left to fend for themselves—like Laurence Jarvik's investigation of American Jewry's response to the holocaust, **Who Shall Live and Who Shall Die**. It was broadcast on "public" television—once in Los Angeles and once in New York, in the late afternoon.

DeMott and Kreines and Jarvik are part of a new generation of nonfiction filmmakers deserving a context far larger than that of television's devouring all-seeing eye. Taking no "reality" for granted, always reaching beneath the surfaces they show, their work might be said to constitute a nonfiction avant-garde, if such a term could be said to be applicable—or necessary.

JOEL DeMOTT and JEFF KREINES.
Joel DeMott: Born in Washington, DC, 1947.
Jeff Kreines: Born in Chicago, 1954.

1969—*Living in the U.S.A.* (16mm, b&w, 4 min.) Jeff Kreines
1970—*Ratamata* (16mm, b&w, 9 min.) Jeff Kreines
1971—*Make-up* (16mm, b&w, 10 min.) Joel DeMott
Ollie & Judy (16mm, b&w, 10 min.) Joel DeMott
Coast-to-Coast/Little Red Hen/Country Chicken/ Golly It's Good (16mm, b&w, 13 min.) Jeff Kreines
McDonald's Is Your Kind of Place (16mm, b&w, 8 min.) Jeff Kreines
His Name Is Wonderful (16mm, b&w, 11 min.) Jeff Kreines
1972—*Thanksgiving* (16mm, b&w, 15 min.) Joel DeMott
Lady Macbeth (16mm, b&w, 15 min.) Joel DeMott
Xmas Film (16mm, b&w, 11 min.) Jeff Kreines

1972—*Pets on Parade* (16mm, color, 8 min.) Jeff Kreines,
   with Tom Palazzolo
   Ricky & Rocky (16mm, color, 16 min.) Jeff Kreines,
   with Tom Palazzolo
   How Much Are You Worth? (16mm, b&w, 18 min.)
   Jeff Kreines
1973—*Mr. Tri-State* (16mm, color, 12 min.) Jeff Kreines,
   with Tom Palazzolo
   Practice/Wedding (16mm, color, 20 min.) Jeff
   Kreines, with Tom Palazzolo
   Enjoy Yourself: It's Later than You Think (16mm,
   color, 22 min.) Jeff Kreines, with Tom Palazzolo
   *Pearl and Seymour Kabaker's 40th Anniversary
   Party at the Artesian Restaurant* (16mm, b&w, 11
   min.) Jeff Kreines
   N.R.A. Wrap-up (16mm, b&w, 7 min.) Jeff Kreines
1974—*Megan* (16mm, color) Joel DeMott
   *The Plaint of Steve Kreines as Recorded by His
   Younger Brother Jeff* (16mm, b&w, 47 min.) Jeff
   Kreines
1975—*Vince and Mary Ann Get Married* (16mm, color,
   36 min.) Joel DeMott and Jeff Kreines
1976—*Montgomery Songs* (16mm, color, 35 min.) Joel
   DeMott and Jeff Kreines
1977—*Down on the Farm* (16mm, color, 50 min.) Joel
   DeMott and Jeff Kreines
   36 Girls (16mm, color, 40 min.) Joel DeMott and
   Jeff Kreines
1978—*God & Country* (16mm, color, 70 min.) Joel DeMott
   and Jeff Kreines
1979—*Goldbug Street* (16mm, color, 90 min.) Joel DeMott
   and Jeff Kreines
   A Simple Trip (16mm, color, 90 min.) Joel DeMott
1980—*Demon Lover Diary* (16mm, color, 90 min.) Joel
   DeMott
1982—*Seventeen* (16mm, color, 120 min.) Joel DeMott
   and Jeff Kreines

The films of Joel DeMott and Jeff Kreines are available
from DeMott/Kreines Films.

In a sense, all our feelings about the cinema revolve around a fundamental deception. The train in Lumiere's **L'Arrivé d'un train en gare de la ciotat** (1896) is universally understood as being real, whereas the one in Méliès's **Voyage à travers l'impossible** (1904) is regarded as false. This is true only insofar as the Lumiere work can claim to have been shot on an actual location whereas the Méliès utilized a painted set. It was, nevertheless, a *real set*. Those first spectators at the Lumiere premiere who (as legend has it) were momentarily frightened into believing that what they saw on screen was about to enter the auditorium quickly recognized this "real" train's falseness. Likewise, those viewers of the Méliès, who in no way believed that the train they saw hurtling through the cinema heavens was doing so in actual life, were nonetheless impressed by the imaginative reality this wish-fulfillment fantasy realized for them.

The history of the cinema has largely been seen in terms of these two trains, one (Lumiere) heading down a track called documentary, the other (Méliès) taking a route labelled narrative fiction. Both, however, move in the same direction as far as the all-encompassing category of cinematic reality is concerned. The "real" of the fiction film is that of a carefully engineered construct—a "language" of shots, camera positions, movements and editing, designed to engender a "suspension of disbelief" so the viewer might share vicariously in the experiences of the characters on the screen. With documentary, on the other hand, the "real" is understood as an *a priori*. We are not asked to enter the world we see on screen, but simply to observe it from a distance. The filmmaker's role is to preserve that distance by minimizing his own role in the process—keeping all traces of his presence as hidden as possible; consequently the documentary filmmaker's duties become every bit as contrived as those of the fiction filmmaker. Despite assumptions of distance, the viewer is just as much involved in the events on screen in a nonfiction work as in a fictional one. And the proof is right up there on the screen.

"Almost everywhere we turn," claim filmmakers Joel DeMott and Jeff Kreines, "documentaries have that same peculiarity—characters who ooze unconsciousness of the camera. People know the medium prefers to keep offstage relations out of the picture and regard camera-consciousness as bad form. That is, they know the appropriate response, the moment the film rolls, is behavior that exudes 'naturalism' through the denial of reality."* To DeMott and Kreines, who for the past 14 years have been working in a *cinéma vérité* mode that would presumably have eliminated such a confused situation, two villains are responsible. First and foremost is what they call the "technical monster" involved in most documentary filmmaking (even some of the *cinéma vérité* variety): "that's how a filmmaker—with his crew, his lights, his loads of equipment—looks to the people he's filming." This obtrusive, gadget-encrusted presence backed up by a technical crew of sound and lighting people appears before the subjects as an adversary force. This "Them and Us" dichotomy produces the second destructive factor cited by DeMott and Kreines—the subject's perception of his or her actual life in fictional terms.

---

*From an unpublished essay "Notes on One-Person Shooting."

"To 'the players' the division is so obvious that shooting conditions in a living room seem exactly like conditions of a movie set." The result, consequently, "evokes associations with the old icons of naturalism—pop movies and story TV." People who play at "ordinary everyday life."

The solution to all of this would appear to be the one-person system of shooting that DeMott and Kreines have developed, much along lines established by such *cinéma vérité* pioneers as Jean Rouch and Michel Brault in the Sixties. A compact unit combining a lightweight camera, sound, and lighting facility all in one, the system allows the filmmaker to face his or her subject on an almost human basis. But DeMott and Kreines don't stop there, for in working toward that sense of humanized technology they cross an essential barrier few *vérité* practitioners have ever truly dealt with.

"Good night, Joel," says the heroine of DeMott and Kreines's **Seventeen** before turning out her bedroom light to go to sleep—blacking out the screen in the process. The moment (which follows a long, rambling monologue) passes quickly and casually—so quickly and casually in fact that most viewers are likely to miss it. But like others in the film, where the unavoidable fact of the camera's presence is acknowledged this scene isn't cute or self-congratulatory (as in Warhol's films). Nor is it a slightly glib way for the filmmakers to get off the hook of voyeurism in the face of the intimate details their film is serving up (as the Maysles Brothers' self-acknowledgment was to some degree in **Grey Gardens**). In **Seventeen** DeMott and Kreines have become part of the landscape they're filming—have put themselves on the line with their subjects. Any notion of "objective reality" is, of course, thrown out the window—which is where it belongs. The filmmakers simply know the difference between *a* truth and *the* truth, and the fact that the cinema is far more disposed to producing the former than the latter.

"Why and for whom do we put the camera amongst people?" asked Jean Rouch. "Strangely enough my first response to this will always be the same 'For myself.' "* An honest enough admission. Still, it leaves open the question of who this "self" might be and how it would operate. "I was not there to get a movie of my experience of being in a patrol car," claimed Stan Brakhage of his film of Pittsburgh police officers, **eyes** (1971), "I was there to get the most naked fix I could manage on what was transpiring."† But this "naked fix" inevitably became Brakhage's "experience of being in a patrol car" as his subsequent remarks on the shooting clearly indicate. Brought to the scene of a suicide, "I got out [of the car] and started photographing the body in the street, and then the homicide department arrived and one of the homicide officers pointed at me and said, 'No, no; you don't take pictures of the body.' And this terrified me of course because we weren't

---

*"The Camera and Man" in *Anthropology—Reality—Cinema*, ed. Mick Eaton (London: BFI, 1979), p. 54.
†"Interview with Richard Grossinger" in *Brakhage Scrapbook*, ed. Robert A. Haller (New York: Documentext, 1983), p. 190.

even officially supposed to be in the car at this point." In short, a complex set of circumstances is revolving about the filmmaker, circumstances to which he or she has no conscious access because all filmmaking efforts are centered on result instead of process. The documentarist can produce an image of an event, but its context remains a mystery.

There is no avoiding the fact that the images we see in a documentary film are simply the reverse of those we *don't* see. The camera can present us only with a frame around one piece of reality. What's left outside that frame influences our view of what's in it, on every conceivable level. Navigating around this is no easy task, but so long as a filmmaker remains aware of it and (more importantly) testifies to this awareness through the film there is no reason to feel our view of things is *entirely* obstructed.

DeMott's **Demon Lover Diary** handles this tricky situation with genuine deftness, despite untoward circumstances. Kreines had been hired on as a cinematographer on a low-budget horror film to be shot in Jackson, Michigan called *The Demon Lover*. DeMott simply came along for the ride—with her camera—in the modest hope that what she might film on this odd job assignment (one of the many they've taken over the years to finance their film projects) might prove interesting. It was, but not in a way DeMott expected.

The Demon Lover was the brainchild of Don Jackson and Jerry Younkins, two factory workers whose long-time dream was to make a gruesome little exploitation quickie. There was nothing special in that in and of itself, but the particulars of their project were another matter. As we come to learn, the film was financed by Don's mortgaging his furniture and Jerry's arranging an industrial "accident" that cost him a finger. Despite this home-grown ingenuity, the two have little in actual filmmaking know-how going for them. They're obsessed with make-up effects—sitting around in one scene jabbering away about how they'll help make the picture a hit. But as for writing and direction their ideas are less certain.

Insufficient planning and obscure, often contradictory, directions to the crew are the usual order of the day, as DeMott follows the shoot's on-again-off-again schedule. After a while Kreines begins to suspect that Don and Jerry expect his technical know-how to come to the rescue—his cinematographic skill magically stepping in to supply the necessary filmmaking ingredients. Eventually a mild degree of friction between Kreines and the novice filmmakers develops into all-out hostility, with Don and Jerry—who, as it turns out, are avid gun collectors as well as horror aficionados—chasing DeMott and Kreines off into the night, rifles blazing.

DeMott's filming of all of this is both lucid and casual. Taking advantage of the soundtrack as an editorial resource she adds, through occasional bits of narration, information both about the general circumstances involved in what we see and hear (what's going on in a specific scene not immediately apparent from the action) and about what happened just prior to a certain

Frame enlargement from *Demon Lover Diary*, by Joel DeMott

shot (unfilmed) that influences what we subsequently see. She informs us of important off-screen events (e.g. shooting the room in which she and Kreines are staying while explaining in voice-over that there was no shooting today because ..., etc.), and even goes into the whys and wherefores of particular shots, such as one scene at a party where she's stationed with her camera in long shot, even though it's a closer shot of a particular individual that she was really trying to get at the time. Altogether, it's a far cry from the likes of Frederick Wiseman, who invariably leaves the viewer up an audiovisual stream without a paddle.

This isn't to say that there aren't any problems on the horizon. DeMott, whose background is urban and sophisticated, is quite open and aboveboard about the social friction that separates her and Kreines from the likes of Don and Jerry. There is no snobbery in any of this. She has simply never met anyone quite like them before, and wasn't prepared for the situation that eventually evolved (on a personal level, cinematically she's fully armed). She's amused that the pair have gotten as far as they have with their hare-brained schemes. Yet when things turn truly difficult she doesn't miss a beat—even to the extent of letting her camera swing toward the ground, the better to aid a hasty getaway when the action gets heated.

The personal problems DeMott and Kreines faced with **Demon Lover Diary** didn't arise during the shooting of **Seventeen**, in no small part because the filmmakers spent over a year filming their subjects—Midwestern teenagers.

Frame enlargement from *Demon Lover Diary*, by Joel DeMott

The difficulty this time came not from within the situation but from without. **Seventeen** was made for PBS television as part of a documentary series called *Middletown.* A catch-all title for a loose umbrella-style grouping of five feature films and one videotape, the *Middletown* series was ostensibly designed to deal with select aspects of life in the modern Midwest. The hook for these six, quite separate productions (which is to say the means by which the project won financial backing from the National Endowment for the Humanities) was *Middletown in Transition*, a sociological study of mid-America written by Robert and Helen Lynd in the Twenties (and later updated in the Thirties). The relationship between the series and the Lynds' research was, to put it mildly, informal. Topics for each film were selected in a manner that on some level might be seen to link up with the alleged source, but no attempt was made to incorporate either the Lynds' research or their methodology. Each film was shot by a different filmmaker or team working independently from one another, utilizing different shooting methods—most, often as not, involving "technical monster" procedures. The only point in common for films in the series was the location: Muncie, Indiana. **The Campaign** dealt with a local election, **Second Time Around** a wedding, **Community of Praise** a church group, **Family Business** a pizza franchise, and **The Big Game** (the videotape) a basketball match. **Seventeen**, as might be gathered, was designed to account for Muncie's youth.

DeMott and Kreines, who had worked for years on films with subjects ranging from a mafia wedding (**Vince and Mary Ann Get Married**) to their own personal lives (**The Plaint of Steve Kreines as Recorded by His Younger Brother Jeff**), without getting any closer to an audience much larger than that of their filmmaking peers, leaped at the opportunity of reaching millions in one fell swoop. They were also heartened by the participation of their teacher, documentary veteran Richard Leacock, on the project. (Leacock's **Community of Praise**, made with Marisa Silver, also rejected "technical monster" methodology.) What they didn't anticipate was the fact that both their subject and their shooting methods would clash with the decidedly conservative designs of PBS and the corporate underwriters that make a series like *Middletown* viable.

Frame enlargement from *Seventeen*, by Joel DeMott and Jeff Kreines

Seventeen centers chiefly on Lynn Massie and her immediate circle of friends, who all attend Muncie's Southside High School. Attractive, funny, vivacious, and more than a bit of a tease, Lynn (who is white) at the film's outset is dating (somewhat clandestinely) one of Southside's black basketball players, John Vance. Outside of this somewhat explosive social circumstance, the two treat one another like countless teenage couples—playful yet guarded, half-adults, half-children. Because of the rapport DeMott and Kreines establish with their subjects, and their sensitivity to nuances of speech, incident, and interpersonal interchange, **Seventeen**'s action moves freely and easily from Lynn's situation to that of her classmates and friends. So sure is the filmmakers' grasp of people and events, that they even move away from Lynn entirely on two occasions. The first concerns Robert House, another black student (in Lynn's home economics class) who has just fathered an illegitimate child. The second more lengthy detour takes in Keith Buck, a white friend of Lynn's whose best friend dies in an auto accident (off-screen) during the shooting.

With DeMott covering the girls, and Kreines the boys, **Seventeen** presents teenagers at their ease without unnecessary fuss or personal prying. Frank, sassy, often quite salty with their language, they are all nonetheless quite aware of and articulate about their personal situations. Because of the filmmakers' commitment to follow their story where it takes them rather than lead it by the nose, a number of fascinating areas involving race and social relations crop up in the film without being forced. (This in and of itself sets DeMott and Kreines's achievement apart from even the best of *cinéma vérité*, which invariably deploys its forces about a highly specified subject (e.g. the political campaign in the classic **Primary**) or personality (Jane Fonda in Leacock's **Jane**).)

We learn quite casually that black students and white students, while able to deal freely with one another on school premises, know that outside its walls lines are firmly drawn, with specific parts of town reserved for each. Further stereotypes are broken in relation to Lynn, who is at heart far from the interracial crusader she might at first glance appear. As we get to know her in the course of the film, it becomes increasingly apparent that her motives for seeing a boy like John are quite mixed—a genuine sense of interest, plus a typical teenage sense of daring in crossing over forbidden lines. Lynn relishes the danger, but when John's black girlfriends begin making threatening phone calls to Lynn's house, she quickly breaks off their relationship.

This break-up, it should be noted, also comes after an incident in which a cross is burned on the lawn of the Massie home. "It was about *so* tall," says Lynn's mother, Shari, shrugging off the affair as a childish prank. Both of Lynn's parents have taken her flirtation with John in surprising stride. They aren't standard-bearers of white liberal upper-middle class virtue, just practical lower-middle class working people with no bones to pick and no phony sense of propriety. They also have a gun in the house if things really get out of hand.

None of this comes across on the screen with any of the sensationalism it might suggest when read here. DeMott and Kreines let their subjects speak for themselves, without added narration, and without pushing any "telling" detail forward, even in intimate scenes, such as one very striking moment when another black friend of Lynn's (obviously deeply in love with her) warns her against seeing John. The one-person shooting method makes the scene, which takes place in a car parked in front of Lynn's house, as intimate as possible. The filmmakers are *right there*—not distanced flies on the wall observing from a safe illusory "outside." This same sense of matter-of-fact immediacy comes through in the film's second half as well, which is dominated by Keith Buck. While at a party at Lynn's, Buck learns that his friend Tim "the churchmouse" has been killed in an automobile accident. As he proceeds to mourn his friend by getting as drunk as an American teenager can, DeMott and Kreines observe his plight with unblinking compassion.

These scenes all become part of a tapestry that DeMott and Kreines, almost inadvertently, have been weaving throughout **Seventeen**. Without any obvious formal plan or program, the filmmakers cover nearly every major adolescent experience—dating rituals, young love (*and* young lust), teenage pregnancy, parental relationships, and death. It is because of this simple honesty that the treatment the film went on to receive is so monstrously unfair.

Seventeen's relationship with the *Middletown* series, as it turned out, was doomed from the very beginning. Series producer Peter Davis had shown a few excerpts from the film, and others in the series, to a representative of the Xerox Corporation in the hopes of getting the sort of financial backing *Middletown* would need to win any degree of public attention. While the rules of public broadcasting forbid interference on an editorial level from "the private sector," it is an open secret that corporate underwriters wield an enormous influence over "public" television. Approval from Xerox would provide only a small amount of actual capital for the series, but at the same time priceless amounts of free advertising would also be involved.

Xerox, however, didn't like what it saw of **Seventeen** (which at that stage was only a brief excerpt, as the film was still in production). Work continued on the series, but as DeMott and Kreines later learned, a backstage maneuver was already underway to keep **Seventeen** out of it. The filmmakers first heard of the trouble on completion of the film when PBS demanded a series of cuts. "Language" was the ostensible chief objection, but according to DeMott and Kreines, PBS was in fact far more concerned with the interracial romance depicted in the film. Scenes involving two brief kisses had to go, as well as a far more "innocent" scene in which Lynn and John and another interracial couple go to an amusement park. The request for this cut clearly tipped the hand of **Seventeen**'s opposition. With that scene gone, it would appear as if Lynn were the only teenage girl in Muncie to take a liking to a black youth.

DeMott and Kreines objected vociferously. But after a preview closed-circuit "feed" of the film to PBS affiliate stations, it became clear that the network was going to have its way. With then PBS President Lawrence Grossman publicly stating to the press his objection to the series, and Xerox representative Bob Schneider calling **Seventeen** a film "we could not suggest parents and students viewing in their own homes," the pressure was on. *Middletown* was aired minus **Seventeen**.

Concurrent with these events was a situation that had sprung up in Muncie itself. Jim Needham, manager of the local PBS affiliate and a well-known right-wing conservative (he once cancelled a documentary on air pollution in favor of an Art Linkletter special pushing for prayer in the public schools), used the feed as a "springboard" for an all-out campaign against **Seventeen**. Private screenings and town meetings were arranged in which the film was attacked as a slur on all of Muncie. Charges flew back and forth in the local media claiming everything from the notion that the film-makers had deliberately singled out the "worst elements" of the community, to the idea that hidden cameras were used. Things even went so far in one incident reported in the Muncie press that one of the teenage girls seen in the film was asked to "confess" that the filmmakers had "put her up" to kissing a black youth.

What was behind all of this was clear enough. Because of the *Middletown* series the film wasn't seen as dealing with individuals and their lives, but as an ideological projection of the community as a whole. The teenagers in **Seventeen** weren't "typical" (read "ideal")—they were neither bland, untroubled, polite, nor obedient. Added to this were the film's disclosures of race and class relations. The film deals with the lower-middle classes, not the upper-middle ones usually deemed suitable to the "typical." In a way, these upset Muncians were like the spectators before Lumiere's train—they thought that what they saw on screen was about to run them over. In a way it was. DeMott and Kreines had lucked out in **Seventeen**. They had stumbled onto the great American subject—race relations. It is not for technique alone that **The Birth of a Nation** is so highly regarded, but for the giddy delight produced by the spectacle of racist hatred, unbridled and unashamed. DeMott and Kreines produce its opposite, in a film that calmly and simply contemplates the reality of an integrated educational system—that the races of their own accord can come together and relate freely and honestly *and* sexually. It is not an easy vision for America to deal with in this particular space and time. But the force of the truths that DeMott and Kreines bring forth cannot be ignored. They constitute a true *Voyage à travers l'impossible* that America must make if its soul can ever hope to heal itself.

LAURENCE JARVIK.
Born in New York City, 1957.

1982—*Who Shall Live and Who Shall Die?* (16mm, b&w, 90 min.)

Distributed by Kino International.

From Stanley Kramer's all-star soap opera, **Judgement at Nuremberg**, to Alain Resnais's lucid essay/meditation **Night and Fog**, the Nazi extermination of six million Jews in the death camps of World War II has been explored many times on the screen. Yet for all its seeming familiarity, the subject has never been regarded in the light provided by Laurence Jarvik's **Who Shall Live and Who Shall Die?** For 90 sobering minutes, this terse, spare documentary feature chooses not to lament the workings of Evil, as so many films have done in the past, but rather to question how those workings might have been minimized and perhaps even halted altogether.

Examining America's reaction to the plight of Europe's Jews from the moment Hitler's loathsome plans were first put into effect to the war's very end, Jarvik's film juxtaposes newsreels of the period with present-day interviews with government officials (Senator Claiborne Pell, Congressman Emmanuel Celler, and War Refugee Board members Josiah DuBois, Ira Hirschmann, Roswell McClelland, and John Pehle) and American Jewish leaders (Nahum Goldman, Gerhart Reigner) in an attempt to discover the truth about the situation. The result is a stinging indictment of the Roosevelt administration's lamentable inability to rise properly to the challenge of the ever-growing tragedy. From antiquated xenophobic immigration quotas to a rather astonishing timidity to undertake such practical maneuvers as the bombing of the camps at Auschwitz (a move that in itself would have saved thousands of lives), the record of too little being done too late is a shocking one. More shocking still is the reaction of the American Jewish community to the situation.

Who Shall Live and Who Shall Die?, by Laurence Jarvik. © 1981 by Blue Light Film Company.

Rather than forming a united front against a common enemy, all manner of factionalism and rivalry broke out amidst groups all claiming to represent that community's best interests. Fear that a demand that the government aid Europe's Jews would lead to an anti-Semitic backlash gripped the American Jewish establishment. Pro-refugee efforts such as the 1943 Rabbi's March on Washington and Ben Hecht's massive propaganda pageant "We Shall Never Die" (produced by Billy Rose at Madison Square Garden in 1944 with music by Kurt Weill and a cast that included Edward G. Robinson, Paul Muni, John Garfield, and Sylvia Sidney) were frowned upon by this leadership faction. Efforts made along the same lines by such controversial Zionist leaders as Peter Bergson (a backer of the Hecht pageant) and Samuel

Merlin (who like Bergson is interviewed in Jarvik's film) were even more vociferously opposed. As the film documents, American Jewish Congress President Rabbi Stephen Wise went so far as to attempt to get Bergson (whom Wise called "a bigger threat to the Jewish people than Hitler") deported.

More than interpersonal bickering and paranoia were involved in all of this, in Jarvik's view. The reaction of the American Jewish establishment clearly cut across class lines. A rescue effort promised these upper-middle class scions nothing less than an influx of interlopers from a class beneath them.

Jarvik's view of this often quite explosive material is measured and fair-minded. From interview to interview, document to document, we are presented one piece of information, one turn of history after another in a line of direct absolute clarity. The beauty found in a work like this is not so much aesthetic as formal. It is the beauty of moral logic as it confronts the most essential issue faced by mankind—responsibility for action.

Since the making of **Who Shall Live and Who Shall Die?** Jarvik has attempted to apply the same moral logic in other areas—principally a project concerning the former secretary of state, **Henry Kissinger: Morality and Power**. Attempts at raising financial backing for this film, which would attempt the exceedingly difficult work of separating myth from actuality in Kissinger's career, have thus far been unsuccessful.

Who Shall Live and Who Shall Die?, by Laurence Jarvik. © 1981 by Blue Light Film Company.

How did you come to make a film like this?
When I was at Berkeley in 1977, James Kurth, a former professor of mine at Swarthmore College, came to me and said "What are you going to do

now?" I was going to graduate in about a year or so. I began talking about my family. On my mother's side they came from Europe—refugees. I started crying. They got out because they had some money, they had some means. People with no money, no means *died.* So Kurth started crying. That's really when I found the theme of my film. I was a philosophy major at Berkeley, but I was dissatisfied with the program there because it was mostly language-analysis oriented. John Searle is the most famous faculty member there. I wasn't interested in that. I was interested in ethics—Good and Evil. This was a very clear example. It's affected other people in other situations long afterward, like in the anti-war movement. People didn't want to be "good Germans" and drew parallels to the Nazis. In Central America today when people are called Nazis it's like ... devils. I was interested in the dynamic in relation to the United States and the Jews.

And you wanted to do it as a film?
Well it started out as a thesis, but then I realized it had to be a film. I had been to California once before—before I came to Berkeley. When I was in high school I was in an internship program and worked with Peter Bart, who at that time was producing **Fun with Dick and Jane**. And I hung out on the set, and watched the editing, and met Max Palevsky.

Did you meet Jane (Fonda)?
I didn't meet Jane, but I met George Segal's wife! Anyway, it didn't look terribly *hard* making films. So then you begin to develop a theory that it's an industrial art, like making cars. You can handcraft a car. Thousands of them are made every day. Film was something people just *did.* It wasn't so mysterious to me anymore.

And you had seen a lot of films.
Oh, yes. I'd organized a festival when I was at Swarthmore called "Real-politik," political films. But my background was more journalistic/historical. I knew **The Sorrow and the Pity** of course, but there were things about it that annoyed me. I felt it was too long and I didn't like the narration. I couldn't have anything like that for my film—I hadn't lived through any of this myself—these weren't my experiences. I didn't want a fake narrator to stand in for me either. That was a piece of advice I took from Emile De Antonio. He said the best documentaries have no narration. But you know I was influenced by a lot of other things as well. When I was at Berkeley I went to the Pacific Film Archive a lot. Werner Herzog and all these other filmmakers came and spoke. In fact, the story of this film in a way could be about how a Jewish boy from New York wanted to become part of this German film movement! (*laughs*) But seriously, it all came about when Jim Kurth gave me the money and told me, literally, "Do anything you want." It started at $25,000 and then it went to $37,000, given to me in increments. It ended up at around $60,000. People have made low-budget features for that.

Obviously in a film like this the editing was the most important part.
Well yes. One day during production I was looking at what was at that
point *hours* of footage with James Kurth and he said to me, "Larry, you've
never been to film school. How are you ever going to make an hour-and-a-
half movie out of this?" And I told him that for the first time in my life I
understood what Michelangelo meant about the statue being in the stone
and you chip away at everything that doesn't look like the statue. That's
how I made it—not as Michelangelo, but that's how I made it. I showed it
to lots of people at early stages when it was terrible, three hours long and
making no sense. I asked about what needed to be shown more, and what
less. I must give full credit to Nancy Strickland on this score. She was with
me from the beginning, helping me with my research and giving me advice
on the editing and everything else.

Where did you think the film would be shown after it was finished?
Not so much on television, but maybe a few theaters and Jewish community
centers. Jewish people like to know what's going on. They don't like their
leaders so much you know—their "so-called" leaders I should say because
they weren't elected. People become "Jewish leaders" through bureaucracy.
There's no legitimacy except in the rabbinate.

Did you know it would be controversial?
The particulars of that I didn't really sense until the end when I was finished
with the film. But I was glad to be attacked by *Commentary.** I despise those
people. The response elsewhere has been very gratifying—showing the film
to people and listening to their reactions.

*So now you've become part of the independent documentary movement in
America. What's your reaction to it?*
It's like stumbling into a club and you don't know the secret handshake.
You aren't wearing the right school tie. You haven't paid your dues. So
some people, just because you're this anomaly, notice you. Others pretend
you aren't there or ask you to leave. I've found out I like journalists a lot,
I like writers a lot. There are a *few* filmmakers I can talk to, but not many.

Why is that? Don't you have common goals?
No. The independent documentary film world is even worse than the regular
film world because basically it's a vanity press outfit for rich kids. Whatever
particular conceits they have, they've gone to the schools that give the
grants—mostly Ivy League. So they get grants from large foundations which
represent the interests of the owners of this country, or they get money from
the government—which also represents the interests of the owners of this
country. And just as in abstract art, you don't find too many calls for the
workers to throw off their Winnebagos. If it's obscure and boring enough
an independent documentary will probably get funded, but if it's going to

---

*See Lucy S. Dawidowicz, "Indicting American Jews," *Commentary*, vol. 75, no. 6 (June 1983),
pp. 36-44. Responses to Dawidowicz's article in *Commentary*, September 1983.

try to reach people in any way … I can honestly say with one or two exceptions I have not seen any really good films funded directly by the National Endowment for the Arts, or the National Endowment for the Humanities. What you get are a lot of films about the Third World made with a very condescending attitude by rich white people with trust funds. And a few minority filmmakers. People have their pet minority artists like they have their Chinese houseboy or their Japanese gardener. The films they make can't be *too* good, or they might become popular and the funder would lose his special control. So, far from aiding minorities, it's exploiting them. Everyone has to work non-union for long hours. Some don't even get paid at all. And these people think "Isn't it wonderful" that they can give a little $10,000 grant to some minority film on some tiny little issue, when what's really needed are large sums of money to combat Hollywood exploitation.

So the film cancels out what good it's working for.
Yes. It's just pious liberal hypocrisy. You can say it's sour grapes if you like. I've never gotten an institutional grant from anyone, because I just can't do it their way. There *are* some talented people out there, but most of it is just "feel good" socialism—like **Rosie the Riveter** and **The Good Fight** and **Seeing Red**. And they never tell the truth about things, like **El Salvador: Another Vietnam**. It bent over backwards to make it look like the rebels aren't Communists, and they're *all* Communists.

But that's because they're afraid of saying that—it's a buzzword.
So what? People are Communists, it's a simple fact. You see that's why the idea of an independent film movement is phony because it's *de*pendent on every level. And rather than being communal it's every man for himself. People will not help each other out, because the whole idea is to be in competition for these grants. If you're going to do that it's better to chuck the whole thing and come out to Hollywood where at least you'll be fighting over millions of dollars instead of paltry little amounts. But you know it's all part of the same thing in a way. A lot of these films get funding from studios. It's sort of like having a farm team, like in baseball. They were integrated before the regular teams. Look, I'm not against any of these people working really, and the film festivals the Independent Feature Project runs are great. I'm not against going Hollywood. It's just the rhetoric; like it's some pious holy struggle.

The shocking thing about the way these documentary films are made and distributed is the audience potential. Practically all of television is documentary. Look at the success of a show like "60 Minutes."
That's because of advertising. You need a sponsor to support your film. In countries like England and France—most European countries—television broadcasts any number of educational and historical documentary films because they feel the public has a right to know. Here in America, Congress

has basically given the airwaves away to private parties. There are some FCC regulations about the "public interest" and so forth, but they don't really amount to anything. Television is afraid of controversy. These stations are run by huge corporations for profit, and have a vested interest in defending the capitalist system, and aren't a friend of the independent any more than Hollywood or anyone else. God—I'm beginning to sound like Trotsky! (*laughs*) Anyway, my film was made purely on the stroke of luck of one completely independent person putting up the cash. That, unfortunately, is the only way these things get made in America. It's not true of Europe because you have a real Left there and political discussion. In America there is no political discussion. I come out of a romantic tradition. It's stupid, but it's what I come out of. I really believe that the truth will set you free and an artist's duty is to bring the truth to people. So I end up sounding like Jeremiah denouncing the world. Things haven't changed much since Jeremiah you know. Technology improves but man remains the same.

With many of these independent documentary films it seems as if everyone is given one chance only. Like Cinda Firestone with **Attica**. *She made it and that was that, it seems.*
Well she has money. But a lot of this is because it's so exhausting to make just one—mostly raising the money is the exhausting part. But you see the way the system is set up they don't want you to make another one.

Is that what's happened to your Kissinger project?
Well I may have bit off more than I could chew. I've sort of put it into a file of future projects. But it's a very complicated subject, and everybody's afraid now because of that suit Westmoreland launched against CBS over that Vietnam documentary. You see that's one of the things about purely aesthetic discussions of film—they're outside of the context film comes from. The financial considerations and the political considerations and the cultural considerations are all linked together. Maybe I'll give it all up and become a press baron. (*laughs*) Yes, that's what I'll do. "I think it would be *fun* to run a newspaper."

OTHER CINEMAS

The limits of cinema aren't those of intelligence or imagination, but exhibition and distribution. Most of the filmmakers discussed in this book cling to a slim margin of quasi-visibility—random museum unspoolings, fugitive film festival bookings. Others fight for whatever space and time the few noninstitution-ridden avant-garde showcases available may have to offer. Then there are those who have nothing to fight for at all. Their names come up from time to time, half-rumors/half-legends. "I hear he/she is supposed to be good," or "Well if you liked *that*, there's supposed to be someone else even better," or "He claims to have been influenced by _____, but none of those films has ever been shown here."

Expressions of exasperation over this sad state of affairs are far more common than practical solutions. But in a way, none may be necessary. As the cinema continues to expand on one end (commerce) and contract on the other (Academe), the possibility of an alternative space opening up eventually seems almost inevitable. Bloated prepubescent fantasy and anal retentive grad school pretentiousness aren't the only viable forms of cinematic desire. It will no doubt take a while for these cultural mastodons to go into their final death throes. Once they do we may all be able to get on to ... other things. Some of those things are related to the filmmakers who follow. In no particular order.

JEAN-DANIEL POLLET is the most shamefully neglected figure in the modern European cinema. "Faced by this world ... vibrating before him, Pollet is content to be, at the viewfinder, on the lookout for poetry," wrote Jean-Luc Godard* of **La Ligne de Mire** (1959), Pollet's first semi-improvised feature. Since then Pollet has made a number of works of all shapes and sizes for both television and theatrical release. **Méditerranée** (1963) is among the most important of them. A collaboration with writer Philippe Sollers, it poses a cryptic/poetic narration against the backdrop of a series of images (ruins, a garden, a girl on a hospital operating table) repeated in varying

---

Godard on Godard (New York: Viking Press, 1972), translation and commentary by Tom Milne, p. 128.

combinations and held for different lengths of time. The result is something along the lines of Hollis Frampton's **Zorns Lemma** (1959), but without the migraine headache the latter almost invariably inspires. **Le Horla** (1966), an equally aleatory work, takes the famous Guy de Maupassant tale of mental breakdown and presents it both in terms of a conventional enactment (by Laurent Terzieff) and as an undramatized reading (shots of a tape recorder playing the narration while floating in a boat across the ocean). In addition, Pollet has made several seemingly more mainstream works—comedies starring Claude Melki. Pollet's episode of **Paris vu par** (1964), **L'Amour c'est gai l'amour c'est triste** (1968), and **L'Acrobate** (1975) all feature this brilliant sensitive/shy performer in the Harry Langdon/Stan Laurel tradition in wistfully romantic tales executed with unerring taste and tact. None of them achieved popular success, though they did add to Pollet's personal lustre as they made him appear a "difficult" filmmaker capable of creating simpler works without "compromise." *Success d'esteme* status is nonetheless a heavy cross to bear.

JEAN ROUCH has been referred to many times throughout this book. Suffice it to say that his contribution to nonfiction filmmaking is of monumental importance. All that is needed now are more frequent opportunities to see films like **Les maîtres fous** (1955), **Moi, un noir** (1957), **La Pyramide humaine** (1959), **Chronique d'un été** (1960), **La Punition** (1960), and **Petit à petit** (1969). His methods of directing non-professional performers in re-enactments of moments of their lives demand the sort of intense scrutiny routinely handed out to figures like Laura Mulvey and Peter Wollen.

RAYMOND DEPARDON is another nonfiction filmmaker of note. His incisive study of news agency photographers, **Reporters** (1981), takes full advantage of Jean-Pierre Beauviala's newly developed lightweight, flexible Aaton camera system. Like DeMott and Kreines, Depardon doesn't shy away from filling the viewer in on the context of the situation he is examining, even to the extent of putting subtitles on the screen as the scene is in progress (a method he uses for an important **Reporters** scene). Other Depardon films include **50.81%** (1974), a study of former French President Valerý Giscard d'Estaing's election campaign; **Numero Zero** (1977); and **Fait Divers** (1982), a study of the police. He is at present working on his first fiction film.

ROBERT FRANK is a familiar name to followers of American avant-garde history for his (and Alfred Leslie's) classic "beat generation" homemovie **Pull My Daisy** (1959). Less familiar is the world-famous still photographer's 1964 feature **Me and My Brother**. A study of poet Peter Orlovky's relationship to his retarded brother Julius, it features both nonfiction scenes of the two (and friend Allen Ginsburg) plus fictional interludes in which Joseph Chaikin and members of his "Open Theater" re-enact this real life story. Familiar but seldom seen is Frank's bizarre memento of a Rolling Stones tour, **Cocksucker Blues** (1972), in which "roadies" and assistants get almost as much attention as Mick and the boys—grossly partying and carrying on. Neither familiar nor notorious are such other Frank works as **Keep Busy** (1975), **Life Dances On** (1980), and **Energy and How To Get It** (1981).

NOËL BURCH's enlightening (and highly entertaining) study of early cinema, **Correction Please** (1981), isn't this film theorist's first attempt at applying his ideas directly to the film strip itself. Throughout the Sixties, Burch (with collaborators André S. Labarthe and Jean-André Fieschi) made a number of contributions to French television's *Cineastes de notre temps* series, combining interviews with filmmakers with carefully selected excerpts from their works. Among those spotlighted by Burch: **Samuel Fuller** (1967), **Marcel L'Herbier** (1968), and **Alain Robbe-Grillet** (1969). The ambition of these films is, of course, simpler than that of **Correction Please**, in which excerpts from early films are intercut with a beautifully acted (and set decorated) mini-drama of spies and secret agents. Hommages to Lang and L'Herbier commingle with Burch's delicate and highly sophisticated detailing of the manner in which the "language" of the cinema developed, from allegedly "theatrical" frontality to an integrated relay of shots, to (as the film's temptress/spy puts the agent under her spell) the arrival of sound. Also more than worthy of note is Burch's (to date) sole fiction film, the 1962 short **Noviciate**. This brief Bresson-influenced study of sado-masochism stars André S. Labarthe and features Annette Michelson as a chic dominatrix.

German filmmaker **KLAUS WYBORNY** is also possessed of a critical bent as regards early cinema. His Super-8 and 16mm works—among them **Dallas Texas/After the Goldrush** (1971) and **The Birth of a Nation** (1973)— sport a sharp awareness of narrative syntax and an appreciation of image grain and texture comparable to some of the finest works of Ken Jacobs and Bruce Conner.

TOM CHOMONT has been making exceedingly short 8 and 16mm films (rarely do they exceed five minutes) since the mid-Sixties. Like Wyborny, Chomont's concerns revolve around light and shape, texture and grain. Nevertheless, narrative aspects slip in as well, especially in relation to what might be called his sexual autobiography (a factor connecting him to Curt McDowell to some degree). **Oblivion** (1969), **Love Objects** (1971), and **Minor Revisions** (1971) are some of his many works.

ANDREJ ZDRAVIC is a Yugoslavian émigré to America whose Super-8 sound films of everything from destroyed buildings (**Home**, 1979) to pieces of discarded newspaper (**Breath**, 1976) vibrate with a sense of the *insolite*— that quality of the real made strange Georges Franju identifies as more powerful by far than the *fantastique*. Lately, in such films as **Where the Coast Meets the Sea** (1981) and **Vsi Sveti** (1982), Zdravic has turned to 16mm.

GEORGE KUCHAR's name has adorned these pages in relation to the works of his student Curt McDowell. But this teacher deserves a large share of attention in his own right. From a career that ranges from such now-legendary 8mm satires made with his twin brother Mike as **I Was a Teenage Rumpot** (1960) and **Pussy On a Hot Tin Roof** (1961), to such solo efforts as **Lust for Ecstasy** (1963), **Corruption of the Damned** (1965), and the classic **Hold Me while I'm Naked** (1966), Kuchar has consistently been a name to conjure with. Sadly, not much conjuring has been done in recent years *vis-à-vis* such equally worthy works as **The Sunshine Sisters** (1973) and **Cattle Mutilations** (1983).

Though his **Abschied von Gestern/Yesterday Girl** (1966) ushered in the New German film renaissance, **ALEXANDER KLUGE** is nowhere near as well known as Fassbinder, Wenders, and Herzog, nor as intellectually revered as Syberberg. Often compared unfavorably—and unfairly—with Godard, Kluge's compendia of short story and essay are a breed apart from those of the intellectually capricious Swiss master. Proceeding from well-established traditions of German high seriousness, Kluge has spun out his own variations on the problems of art and social responsibility and the relation of the individual to historical forces in such challenging works as **Die Artisten in der Zirkus-kuppel: Ratlos/Artists under the Big Top: Perplexed** (1968) and **Gelegenheitsarbeit einer Sklavin/Part-Time Work of a Domestic Slave** (1974). His most recent feature, **Die Macht der Gefühle/ The Power of Emotions** (1983), confronts the meaning of art (particularly opera) and the culture that surrounds it through a startlingly loose form involving documentary, first-person essay, and short dramatic interludes. Shot without a script over several years it is a work of near-unprecedented freedom—and intellectual depth. A lawyer, novelist, and theorist of the cinema, Kluge is a firm believer in intellectual power, striving to make works that come to being "in the head of the spectator." In an important essay, "Film and the Public Sphere" (translated in *New German Critique* #24/25, Fall/Winter 1981-1982), Kluge states, "Understanding a film completely is conceptual imperialism which colonizes its subject. If I have understood everything then something has been emptied out."

In 1974 Armenian filmmaker **SERGEI PARADJANOV** was arrested by Soviet authorities on charges of homosexuality (a legal offense in that nation-state), illegal money dealings, and "incitement to suicide." After several years in a forced labor camp, Paradjanov was released—in a manner of speaking. He currently resides under a form of house arrest in his native home of Tbilisi, Georgia. His "crimes," to those familiar with the case, are largely connected with his art. When Paradjanov's 1964 feature **Shadows of Forgotten Ancestors** was released it won instant international acclaim, with comparisons made to the finest works of Eisenstein and Dovzhenko. But the *sotto voce* support of Armenian nationalism in the face of the Soviet state latent in that epic Carpathian folktale became even stronger in Paradjanov's next (and to date last) work, **Sayat Nova/The Color of Pomegranates**. No comparisons to any filmmaker were made with this work, which was shot in 1969 though it surfaced only in the mid-Seventies in cut form. Ostensibly the story of the life of a medieval painter and poet, Paradjanov's film has no narrative as such. One beautiful, mysterious scene follows another in a visual style owing more to painting than cinema. Figures representing the hero and his muse stand in *tableaux vivants*. Shots of water-soaked books and manuscripts blowing in an eerie wind atop a village roof. Figures whose identities are by no means clear (nor do they need be) stare from the screen in lushly colored compositions. "It is a film that has given me a lot of faith in myself," said Jean-Luc Godard, "since it confirmed some ideas I had about film technique.... I think you have to live at least fifteen miles away and feel the need to walk there on foot to see it."*

And then there are *other* cinemas ...

ORSON WELLES.
Born in Kenosha, Wisconsin, 1915.

1934—*Hearts of Age* (16mm, b&w, 6 min.)
1941—*Citizen Kane* (35mm, b&w, 119 min.)
1942—*The Magnificent Ambersons* (35mm, b&w, 88 min.)
1946—*The Stranger* (35mm, b&w, 95 min.)
1948—*The Lady from Shanghai* (35mm, b&w, 87 min.)
          Macbeth (35mm, b&w, 107 min.)
1952—*Othello* (35mm, b&w, 95 min.)
1955—*Mr. Arkadin/Confidential Report* (35mm, b&w, 99 min.)
1958—*Touch of Evil* (35mm, b&w, 108 min.)
          The Fountain of Youth (35mm, b&w, 27 min.)
1962—*The Trial* (35mm, b&w, 120 min.)
1966—*Chimes at Midnight/Falstaff* (35mm, b&w, 115 min.)
1968—*The Immortal Story* (35mm, color, 58 min.)
1975—*F for Fake* (35mm, color, 85 min.)
          F for Fake Trailer (35mm, color, 12 min.)

*Gideon Bachmann, "In the Cinema It Is Never Monday," *Sight and Sound*, Spring 1983.

1978—*Filming Othello* (16mm, color, 85 min.)
Unfinished and/or unreleased films:
1941-42—*It's All True*
1955-75—*Don Quixote*
1967-70—*The Deep*
1970-72—*The Other Side of the Wind*
1978—*The Dreamers*
1980—*Filming the Trial*
in preparation: The Cradle Will Rock

Most of Orson Welles's films are available from
Janus Films and Films Inc. *F for Fake* is a
Newline Cinema release, and *Touch of Evil* is
available from Universal 16.

Orson Welles in a book about avant-garde and independent film? Surely
this is the height of critical capriciousness. This is not the first time Welles's
name has appeared on these pages, however (*see* the sections on Raul Ruiz,
Luc Moullet, Sally Potter, Laurence Jarvik). And who better than Welles to
trace the split that separates Art from Commerce—the division of film from
potential spectator that so troubles the avant-garde? For years Welles has
run the length of that split, beginning with that ceaselessly rhapsodized
blaze of cultural/commercial glory that was and is **Citizen Kane** and continuing over a series of less felicitously engineered undertakings. Viewed alternately (and sometimes simultaneously) as pathetic and heroic, Welles has
drifted across the decades from film to film, making do with inadequate
financing and substandard production arrangements (**Macbeth, Othello**),
accepting a purely commercial assignment or three (**The Stranger, The Lady
from Shanghai, Touch of Evil**), somehow getting made a few films he truly
cared about (**Chimes at Midnight, The Immortal Story**), all the while keeping
close at hand a small stash of even more personal works, unfinished and/or
unreleased (**Don Quixote, The Deep, The Other Side of the Wind**). But
there should be no distinguishing between these films à la Sitney on Kirsanoff;
Welles "made" all of them.

"Always achieving failure, yet bringing it off brilliantly," wrote Parker
Tyler in an essay not insignificantly entitled "Orson Welles and the Big
Experimental Film Cult" (*Film Culture* #29, Summer 1963). For experiment
has been the cornerstone of Welles's work. In Tyler's eyes this places him
in a far from dishonorable commercial tradition that includes (among others)
Griffith, Stroheim, Lang, and Sternberg. All were (Tyler again) "masters of
a *potential* art," making themselves heard above the din of the marketplace
at random moments—all anyone has any right to expect, things being as
they are. Yet the suspicion persists that Welles isn't necessarily part of this
company. For the aberration of **Kane** (and a few others) aside, the majority
of his films have been made under conditions not at all dissimilar to those
of the other filmmakers represented in this book. Making that view viable,

however, requires (as always with Welles) some degree of dealing with the curse and the blessing that **Kane** has become.

"One of the few films ever made inside the United States *in freedom*," declared Pauline Kael in her famous praising-with-not-so-faint-damnation exercise "Raising Kane," "not merely freedom from interference, but freedom from the routine methods of experienced directors." What this "freedom" meant in actual practice, however, wasn't nearly so unprecedented. That routine, unimaginative production methods were (and are) the Hollywood rule cannot be denied, but also undeniable are the exceptions that keep the rule operable—the Griffiths, the Stroheims, the Chaplins, the Sternbergs, etc. In a sense, their techniques were far more radical than Welles's, who after all kept to a reasonable budget and shooting schedule and turned out a relatively standard-length feature. What these predecessors provided was the context that from a purely commercial standpoint made the "freedom" of **Kane** possible.

"The first million dollar picture," crowed Universal over **Foolish Wives** (1922), when it realized that what was going on behind the camera was just as exploitable as what was being placed in front of it. Gleefully they reported every alleged "outrage" of the flamboyant, extravagant Stroheim— even inventing a few along the way. In Welles, RKO obviously saw the same sort of attraction. With his Mercury players he had just scared a gullible nation into half-believing that Martians had landed, in his famous radio broadcast of *War of the Worlds*. This new story satirizing newspaper baron William Randolph Hearst would surely fill the bill in the same spirit. The fact that Welles was taking full advantage of the studio's technical resources for a film that in its final state would contain far in excess of the usual number of trick or process shots seen in the average feature also was seen as a bonus. In order for this project to work at all it would have to look as different from the run of the Hollywood mill as possible. That the studio's enthusiasm for Welles subsequently cooled, however, is attributable to a number of factors—**Kane** itself in all likelihood being the least of them.

Though Hearst and his associates had tried to stop the film dead in its tracks, managing only to keep it out of playing more theaters than it might initially have appeared in, it proved to be a modest commercial success. The reviews were unstinting in their praise of Welles *and* RKO for having the foresight to hire him. But in the period immediately following **Kane** things were moving along quite different lines, with Welles following the **Kane** sensation with the calmer, less commercial (and more incisive, and more personal, and more profound) **The Magnificent Ambersons**. At the same time, he was also embroiled in the episodic semi-documentary about jazz and Latin culture, **It's All True**, and was overseeing **Journey into Fear** (produced and co-written by, and featuring Welles, but directed by his associate Norman Foster). This last mentioned project, the most conventional of the trio, was completed and released more or less as planned. **Ambersons**, however, was halted prior to the completion of scenes Welles felt were crucial to its conception, and cut into final shape over his objections. **It's All True** was halted by the studio altogether and never finished.

Welles's next filmmaking opportunity didn't come until 1945 with **The Stranger**, his only *truly* ordinary work to date. According to Welles, this standard-issue my-husband's-trying-to-kill-me melodrama, with a *soupçon* of social consciousness (the husband in question is a Nazi) was made in order to prove that he could go the routine route. Welles may merely have been trying to save face, for his next film, based on equally unpromising material, was **The Lady from Shanghai** (begun in 1946 but not released until 1948). Starring his then-just-ex-wife Rita Hayworth, this flamboyant melodrama about the rich and ruthless came to be made when Welles's fortunes in the theater, to which he had returned after his initial Hollywood sojourn, turned sour with the ill-fated stage production of *Around the World in 80 Days*. In need of work, Welles took on this Columbia release, which while cut by hands other than his own, was universally recognized (and heralded) as his film in spirit and substance. Had Welles wished it, he could have had a perfectly respectable career as a gentleman hack much on the order of his friend and collaborator John Huston—whose impressive first feature **The Maltese Falcon** debuted to great acclaim the same year as **Kane**. Welles, however, was veering off in another filmmaking direction.

He followed **The Lady from Shanghai** not with another potboiler, but with a hastily (and ingeniously) slapped together version of **Macbeth**, shot in 23 days for Republic Studios on the set of an old Tex Ritter western, using costumes borrowed from an opera company. The results have been likened by most critics to more of a "rough sketch" of Shakespeare's play than a completed work. But it served notice that Welles's directorial career was heading away from the mainstream and toward the margins. This fact became even clearer with his next work, **Othello**, which marks the *real* beginning of his filmmaking and defines the real Orson Welles.

Begun in 1949, **Othello** didn't reach the light of the motion picture screen until 1952, due to a truly unprecedented series of circumstances. Financed on a shoestring, the production was forced to shut down not long after it began. There's nothing unusual in this in the motion picture world, where all manner of cinema sits about half-finished and rotting in cans or thrown unceremoniously into the garbage. The unprecedented part is Welles's refusal to let **Othello** die. Taking acting jobs and putting his earnings back into the film he continued to shoot it off and on, slowly but surely putting the bits and pieces together. The result was an even rougher sketch than **Macbeth**, but a work that is far more beautiful. Scenes from the play unfold in any number of locations—Rome, Venice, Morocco—and were welded together in the editing room. Forced to cover spatio-temporal gaps at every turn out of necessity, Welles turned this disadvantage into an emblem of style. "Iago changed continents in the middle of a phrase," Welles noted in **Filming Othello**, his 1978 documentary-essay on the making of the film. The sense of wonder latent in the remark is in every way justified. Here was a film that wasn't a simple re-enactment of Shakespeare's play, but an original work in and of itself. Inability to "match" voice with image made it possible for both elements to float free—Shakespeare's poetry and Welles's imagery working both separately and together as a true image/sound dialectic every bit as complex and resonant as Godard's **Prénom: Carmen**.

"When Welles went to Europe, he lost his single greatest asset as a movie director: his sound," complained Pauline Kael,* to whom Wellesian sound was synonymous with the style he had developed in radio and simply transferred to film for **Kane** and **Ambersons**. The sound of **Othello** was of another order, with Welles himself doubling and tripling for players who for one reason or another couldn't be there for post-production to speak for themselves. The poetic possibilities of an Othello and an Iago speaking with the same voice were scarcely lost on someone like Welles, who went on to utilize such audiovisual non-conformity again and again. One of the most striking examples occurs in **Touch of Evil**, Welles's first Hollywood film since **Macbeth** and a production that while far from lavish wasn't wanting on a basic technical level. Accosted on a streetcorner early in the action by a youth she calls "Pancho" (Valentin de Vargas), Janet Leigh finds herself surrounded by a group of Mexican passersby. Not understanding the Spanish with which he addresses her, she asks for help. These passersby all speak with the voices of Welles and Akim Tamiroff—aurally prefiguring their physical encroachment on Leigh in the film's second half.

This may seem a minor thing—a private joke from Welles to Welles (and a few select others). But looking over a career that is filled with such moments provides a far different picture. For like Melville, Resnais, and Rivette, Orson Welles is one of the cinema's great cryptographers. References and cross-references wend their way from work to work forming a network of ciphers of near-Borgesian proportions. And not only those works Welles alone has signed are involved. Idle rumors to the effect that Welles directed a number of films in which he appeared (**Jane Eyre** the most frequently cited example) aren't the point, but rather those where the Wellesian persona was made truly to matter. This is the case with **The Third Man**, which he did not direct, and with **Follow the Boys** (Edward Sutherland, 1944), in which he obviously had more than a small hand. The sequence in question involves Welles as a magician and Marlene Dietrich as his assistant. Sawing Dietrich in half, utilizing methods that are purely cinematic in nature (her legs dance off the screen by themselves), creates a key Wellesian moment. The scene is a reference to their off-screen friendship. Years later it provides

---

Kiss Kiss Bang Bang (New York: Atlantic - Little, Brown, 1968), p. 196.

a context for Dietrich's appearance in **Touch of Evil**. A still photograph of Welles and Dietrich in **Follow the Boys** appears in **F for Fake** at the beginning of a segment devoted to Welles's Hollywood career. This is as it should be, for Welles's prime persona, as **Follow the Boys** underscores, is that of a *magician* of cinema.

Film analysis, be it semiotically oriented or otherwise, always seems to turn on thematic matters. In Welles's case these are simply stated: his films almost always center on a conflict between two men over a woman. One man (consciously or unconsciously) seeks to destroy the other who (also consciously or unconsciously) seeks to be destroyed. Prime examples (in order) being: **Othello, Mr. Arkadin, Touch of Evil, The Immortal Story, F for Fake**. In this context **Citizen Kane** is somewhat stillborn. Had the reporter Thompson (William Alland) not been a faceless audience surrogate but an active character, falling in love with Susan Alexander Kane after hearing her pathetic tale (not an unreasonable set of circumstances—the basic set-up is all there and ready to go), **Kane** might have been the disturbing work it desperately wants to be. This reportorial indiscretion would inevitably have brought with it the violation of class lines (Thompson crossing over them as it were, not into the present, but into the imagined past of the rich). This violation forms the core of **Mr. Arkadin**, Welles's correction of the **Kane** scenario in which the magnate in question (played by Welles himself) is alive, but seeks to render his past dead—a project he accomplishes by means of a hired investigator who eventually becomes his antagonist. This criminal ne'er-do-ill, Van Stratten (Robert Arden), falls in love with his employer's daughter—the party for whom this past is being systematically eliminated. Behind it all stands the shadow of the incestuous desire Arkadin harbors for this innocent maiden—evoked by Welles much in the manner of Perrault's "Peau d'Ane," replete with references to ogres and fairy tale castles. But behind this artifice is the undisguised implication that social climbing (Van Stratten's "crime") is every bit the equal of incest (Arkadin's) on the overall scale of things. Adding to the stew is the fact that Arkadin's real background is continually being revealed by the story as not that of the aristocratic Onassis-style jet-setter, but rather that of the shady underworld black marketeer.

It would be possible to go on studying this scenario *ad infinitum* as it appears in film after film, permutation after permutation. But in a very real sense it's all something on the order of a Wellesian red herring—a distraction to aid the magician in his task. For it is process rather than product—or rather process *as* product—that is most central to Welles, and marks his stature as a filmmaker, having far more in common with a Rainer or Kluge (not to mention a Ruiz) than he does with the likes of Huston or Losey. And the crux of it all is magic.

"I was in that room just a minute ago, and that box was empty," wails Charlton Heston to Welles in **Touch of Evil** in the scene where two sticks of dynamite "magically" appear in a suspect's room, implicating him in a murder. Heston's stuffed-shirt of a government official locks horns with Welles's unscrupulous cop in a basic rendition of the thematic formula outlined above. But even more evident is a propensity for sheer prestidigitation. A Mexican border town is conjured out of the streets and alleyways of Venice, California. In **The Trial** the ruins of a railway station are similarly used to stand in for a nightmarish law court of sky-high ceilings and enormous hallways. Standing on the steps of a building on the outskirts of Paris (though identified as those of the court/railway station in the action), Anthony Perkins crosses the street into … Zagreb, Yugoslavia. He turns to address a figure still locked spatio-temporally into Paris.

That all this perpetual motion has a method becomes most clear in **F for Fake**—a film that in many ways Welles had been leading toward (personally and cinematically) for years. It is a film without a genre. There are stories in it, but it has no overall one to tell itself. The cinematic space it offers (*pace* Peter Gidal) is no larger than that of the screen itself. Taking a documentary by François Reichenbach, Welles makes a film in which every image is first and foremost *an image*. We are not fooled into believing anyone we see on screen is *there* in the sense of image relay created by ordinary fiction. But we are fooled nonetheless—or rather, we are *fooled with* by Welles.

The subject of **F for Fake** is nothing more than a lightweight anecdote—the sort of thing Welles would relate on one of his talk show appearances. Reichenbach was making a documentary on art forger Elmyr DeHory, who had been the subject of a biography called *Fake!* written by Clifford Irving. Not long after the shooting, Irving gained international notoriety as the alleged author of what was eventually exposed as a fake biography of billionaire Howard Hughes. Welles speculates on the possible connections between Irving and DeHory, one a student of the other, as it were, in the art of fakery. And in the Wellesian scheme of things the two pair off as well, like Arkadin and Van Stratten. The woman involved enters the film in an extremely indirect fashion in the form of actress Oja Kodar, around whom Welles constructs a blatantly false anecdote about her alleged grandfather, the supposed "king of all the art forgers" and *his* faking, with her help, of a series of Picasso paintings. Over, under, and everywhere in between is Welles himself, adding bits and pieces of his own myth via the fact that he too can claim connection to Hughes, as the latter was Welles's original satirical target in what came to be **Citizen Kane** before he decided to "change tycoons."

With shaggy dog story piling atop shaggy dog story, the patience of the literal-minded is severely tested in **F for Fake**. But for those who've been paying attention, the film's rewards are everywhere apparent. For once Welles puts his ideas right out on the surface—appearing in the opening scene as a magician. In a railway station (recalling **The Trial**) he changes a key to a coin before a small boy's delighted eyes, all the while addressing him and us (the verbal tense and visual direction in which Welles speaks constantly change) as other images shift about the scene. Oja Kodar opens the window of a train compartment to observe Welles from one angle. From another, François Reichenbach and his crew stand filming from a concealed position. "Up to your old tricks again?" Kodar asks of Welles. As he finishes his act she leaves the scene, a fact commented on by Reichenbach. Welles promises that more concerning her will come in time. This scene is the only one in the film in which some semblance of standard cinematic spatio-temporal coordination is observed. After that we have only the screen, with the words of Welles to guide us along. As a result, the subject under discussion is less Irving, or DeHory, than the nature of cinematic reality and the roles Welles has played (and continues to play) in its production.

Shifting between images placed directly on the screen to images of the same activities seen on a movieola (images of images) Welles underscores the fundamental instability of the act of representation itself. Using the sort of montage editors turn to as a last resort to cover visual weak spots, Welles transforms it into a central element of style. He is seen, for example, walking down a side street in Ibiza, where most of the action (if such a word can be used) is set (if such a word can be used). Glancing off-screen, he refers to Clifford Irving "over there," whereupon he cuts to a shot of Irving coming down a street in the direction presumably opposite the one Welles is facing. Then Welles's voice on the soundtrack is heard referring to Elmyr DeHory, who is seen in the shot that follows coming down, one is encouraged to infer, the opposite side of the same street. Welles means to fool no one by this imaginary convergence, only to underscore the way we are fooled, as a matter of course in most films, and the fact that we *wish* to be fooled. Bringing things together and taking them apart is central to the magician's art. The effect created depends on which things are brought together and in which order. With the filmmaker it is exactly the same. The process of folding images and sounds over one another—displaying yet at the same time concealing the film's means of production—runs throughout **F for Fake** (whose telling French title is **Vérités et mensonges**—Truth and Lies). The railway station scene serves as something on the order of a working model for Welles.

An image of an innocent bystander watching Welles's act from the sidelines of that scene sparks the next sequence, a montage of faces caught unaware, this time observant of the spectacle of Oja Kodar as she walks down a series of European streets. Two types of magic-related diversions are involved here. On the one hand there's the one Welles mentions in the film's narration. Through Kodar and the hidden cameras he has made passing strangers "act" for him. The other diversion is the one the sequence itself creates for *us* in the audience. Kodar, Welles informs us, is "bait," but the trap she's connected to is to be "saved for later." We are in short being

Gary Graver in *F for Fake*,
by Orson Welles

"let in" on one deception while another is in progress—the scene diverts us precisely at the point at which we may begin to wonder where Welles and his railway magic tricks are heading.

There is an additional factor involved in this deception. The sequence, Welles tells us, is from "quite another film." What this "other film" might be we can only guess, but alert Wellesians are sure to recognize the implications of the scene that follows, again with Kodar, again referred to by Welles as a scene from "yet another film." In this "gag"(Welles's term), the director/star is shown fitting Kodar (shades of **Follow the Boys**) magically into a tiny trunk. The gag's source is evidently **The Deep**, as Laurence Harvey (Kodar's co-star with Welles and Jeanne Moreau in that still-unfinished film) is present during its execution. What Welles is up to with this odd interpolation may be some form of laying certain of his unfinished works to public rest—creating imaginary spaces where their existence might be noted and filed (much on the order of Rivette's cryptic references to his unfinished

Scènes de la vie parallèle series in **Merry Go Round** and **Le Pont du nord**). But then again this may simply be a way of indicating the infinite number of possible spaces a director/magician might choose to conjure out of film's thin beam of projected air. For in addition to the bits mentioned above, there is also the **F for Fake Trailer**—a 12-minute slice of Wellesian bravura designed (presumably) to explain the film it serves, but made up entirely of original images having no connection to **F for Fake** itself. But—like Welles—we digress....

With the completion of these ceremonial introductions, **F for Fake** gets down to business in its principal setting—Welles's editing table. Rather than create stability, this presumed center quickly erupts into controlled chaos with distractions, diversions, and spatio-temporal interpolations coming thick and fast as the film is stopped, started, reversed, broken apart, and put back together before our eyes. Our only anchor? The *voice* of Orson Welles.

Welles has more on his mind than simple offhand bravura in all of this fancy image shuffling. To Pauline Kael's charge that he in effect stole a film from its rightful owner—**Kane** in her view being almost exclusively the work of co-scriptwriter Herman J. Mankiewicz—Welles offers up an obviously purloined property. The heart of **F for Fake** is outtakes from a documentary shot by François Reichenbach. The process by which Reichenbach's footage becomes Welles's own through editing and narration is no doubt lost on the likes of Kael, who tends to regard film direction as little more than the equivalent of theater staging, a work's content being its written script alone and any other artistic grace notes left over being attributable to the cinematographer and art direction crew. How these areas might be coordinated by a director into a smoothly functioning whole, and the effect this coordination might have on the process of cinematographic writing (the means by which a Welles's work might be distinguished from, say, that of Edward Sutherland) are a total mystery to her.

Welles's detailing of DeHory's evolution from unsuccessful artist to successful art forger, "turning disappointment into a gigantic joke," unavoidably turns on the "joke" of Welles's own career. Confessing to "forging" an American reputation in order to break onto the stage in Europe ("I began at the top and I've been working my way down ever since"), Welles goes on to speak of his most celebrated "forgery"—his "War of the Worlds" radio broadcast. Scaring a sizable part of 1938 America into believing that men from Mars were taking over the country, Welles's Halloween prank paid off in career terms. "I didn't go to jail," he confesses, "I went to Hollywood." Working in a town in which fakery was the order of the day would appear to be ideal for Welles, but it was—as his remark suggests—a prison of sorts (albeit a gilded one). The fakery that most interested Welles—the fakery of art—had its limits in Hollywood. Outside of it he was free—as the finale of **F for Fake** demonstrates.

In it, Oja Kodar returns, walking toward Welles in a fog-enshrouded area identified (on the soundtrack) as Orly airport. The flight we are about to take with them is a thoroughly imaginary one, involving as it does the story (promised at the film's outset) of Kodar's alleged involvement with her grandfather ("the king of all the art forgers," according to Welles) in bilking Pablo Picasso out of a set of his paintings. Here Welles plays his trump card. The story is patently false, yet in terms of the whole of **F for Fake**—riddled as it is with material not "genuinely" Welles's—it is the most *authentic* sequence. True to Kael's insistence on the importance of Welles's radio origins, the aural predominates—the voice of Welles is all over the place; he has "his sound" more than ever before. We see Kodar walking through streets, much as she did earlier, this time serving as bait to ensnare Picasso—represented by several black and white photographs. This is no documentary, no attempt at *cinéma vérité*. We are at no point made to believe that Picasso is actually *present* in an artificially contrived *mise-en-scène* that makes the "look" of the photos appear to be directed Kodar's way. We *are* misled, however, when the scene shifts back to its original fog-bound setting. "May I call you Pablo?" says Welles, addressing Kodar as the two serve as stand-ins for an exchange that allegedly took place between Picasso (here played by Kodar) and Kodar's grandfather (played by Welles). The confusion matters little, for by this point all sense of identity has been thoroughly undermined. We do not know who or what to believe—and we don't have to. Soon space itself disappears as the "airport" is revealed to be a movie studio set. Still, Welles assures us that some sense of reality is apprehensible. The only trouble is it has nothing to do with art. "Reality is the toothbrush waiting at home for you in the glass, a bus ticket, a paycheck, and the grave," he tells us with solemnity. A cheerful farewell to both his images and the audience quickly follows.

That Welles chose to release this film prior to the ones he's been storing away like winter provisions for some long dark night of the soul, is of course of considerable significance. Clearly Welles feels it necessary that an audience know how to read images it it's ever going to understand the likes of a **Don Quixote**. A transposition of Cervantes's tale to the modern world, pitting the legendary knight against steam shovels, atom bombs, and—most important of all—movie screens, it is a project that has absorbed Welles since 1955. "It's really finished," Welles told interviewers for a Spanish cinema magazine in 1964, "It only needs about three weeks' work in order to shoot several little things. What makes me nervous is launching it: I know that this film will please no one. This will be an execrated film and I need a big success before putting it in circulation. If **The Trial** had been a complete success, then I would have had the courage to bring out my **Don Quixote**."*

---

*Juan Cobos, Miguel Rubio, and Jose Antonio Pruneda, "Interview with Orson Welles," originally published in *Film Ideal*, reprinted in *Cahiers du cinéma* #165 (April 1965), p. 35.

Promotional image for *F for Fake*

Mr. Arkadin

F for Fake indicates that Welles's attitudes have changed since those words were spoken. It is not the film of a man in search of success, but rather one of a filmmaker content with his status as perpetual outsider. No more fighting with Hollywood, no more challenging Europe. Instead Welles presents something neither can offer—a diversion. **F for Fake** is a genuine rarity—a modest film from a less than modest man. All it wants is to help us pass an evening's leisure time pleasantly. The only problem is such diversions have little place in the post-Spielberg era.

As the film spills out across a screen, all the contradictions of a career that matched resolute integrity on one level (filmmaking) with wholesale "selling out" on the other (the "Dean Martin Celebrity Roasts," films like **The Tartars** and **Butterfly**) fold over one another. All that's left is for Welles to fess up and admit to being what he's been since **Othello**—a thoroughly independent filmmaker. All that's left for us is to ponder the prospect of **Don Quixote**—a myth of the cinema second only to the complete **Greed**.

Filmed by Welles with a crew consisting at times only of the performers, his then wife (Paola Mori), and his chauffeur (who handled the lights), it was made in fits and starts. Today the leading players—Francesco Reiguera (Quixote) and Akim Tamiroff (Sancho)—are dead. But like Jack Smith's endlessly edited projects, Welles's film lives on. Periodically an announcement comes forth. We're told it will be ready "soon." We can wait. For as what's now known as the cinema continues to wrest itself out of shape, moving farther away from any semblance of a satisfactory form with which to deal with audience desire, **Don Quixote** looms on the horizon as the first important attraction of what might be called the post-cinematic era. And it is in this arena—our *future* avant-garde—that Orson Welles may finally truly become ... our obedient servant.

"I await the end of cinema with optimism."
—Jean-Luc Godard

APPENDIX: Distributors

American Federation of Arts
41 East 65th St.
New York, NY 10021

British Film Institute
29 Rathbone St.
London W1P 1AG
ENGLAND

Canyon Cinema Cooperative
Room 220
Industrial Center Building
Sausalito, CA 94965

DeMott/Kreines Films
5330 Kennedy Ave.
Millbrook, AL 36054

Film-Makers' Cooperative
175 Lexington Ave.
New York, NY 10016

Les Films du Passage
22 rue Faubourg du Temple
Paris
FRANCE

Filmverlag der Autoren
1 Smaningerstrasse 65
8 Munich 80
GERMANY

First Run Features
419 Park Ave., South
New York, NY 10016

**L'Institut National de la
    Communication Audiovisuelle**
Tour Gamma A-193
197 rue de Bercy
Paris 12 eme
FRANCE

Janus Films/Films Inc.
440 Park Ave., South
New York, NY 10016

5625 Hollywood Blvd.
Los Angeles, CA 90088

Kino International
250 West 57th St.
New York, NY 10019

London Filmmakers Cooperative
42 Gloucester Ave.
London W1
ENGLAND

Luc Moullet
27 rue Timbaud
75011 Paris
FRANCE

Munic Film
Friedrich-Herschel-Strabe 17
8000 Munich 80
GERMANY

Museum of Modern Art
11 West 53rd St.
New York, NY 10019

New Line Cinema
853 Broadway
New York, NY 10003

Jack Smith
21 First Ave., #33
New York, NY 10003

Universal 16
445 Park Ave.
New York, NY 10022

Name Index

Film Title Index